African History: A Very Short Introduction

Very Short Introductions available now:

PRESOCRATIC PHILOSOPHY
    Catherine Osborne
PSYCHOLOGY   Gillian Butler and
    Freda McManus
PSYCHIATRY   Tom Burns
QUANTUM THEORY
    John Polkinghorne
RACISM   Ali Rattansi
THE RENAISSANCE   Jerry Brotton
RENAISSANCE ART
    Geraldine A. Johnson
ROMAN BRITAIN   Peter Salway
THE ROMAN EMPIRE
    Christopher Kelly
ROUSSEAU   Robert Wokler
RUSSELL   A. C. Grayling
RUSSIAN LITERATURE
    Catriona Kelly
THE RUSSIAN REVOLUTION
    S. A. Smith
SCHIZOPHRENIA
    Chris Frith and Eve Johnstone
SCHOPENHAUER
    Christopher Janaway
SHAKESPEARE
    Germaine Greer

SIKHISM   Eleanor Nesbitt
SOCIAL AND CULTURAL
    ANTHROPOLOGY
    John Monaghan and Peter Just
SOCIALISM   Michael Newman
SOCIOLOGY   Steve Bruce
SOCRATES   C. C. W. Taylor
THE SPANISH CIVIL WAR
    Helen Graham
SPINOZA   Roger Scruton
STUART BRITAIN   John Morrill
TERRORISM
    Charles Townshend
THEOLOGY   David F. Ford
THE HISTORY OF TIME
    Leofranc Holford-Strevens
TRAGEDY   Adrian Poole
THE TUDORS   John Guy
TWENTIETH-CENTURY
    BRITAIN   Kenneth O. Morgan
THE VIKINGS   Julian D. Richards
WITTGENSTEIN   A. C. Grayling
WORLD MUSIC   Philip Bohlman
THE WORLD TRADE
    ORGANIZATION
    Amrita Narlikar

Available soon:

1066   George Garnett
ANTISEMITISM   Steven Beller
CITIZENSHIP   Richard Bellamy
CLASSICAL MYTHOLOGY
    Helen Morales
EXPRESSIONISM
    Katerina Reed-Tsocha
GEOPOLITICS   Klaus Dodds
GERMAN LITERATURE
    Nicholas Boyle

HUMAN RIGHTS
    Andrew Clapham
INTERNATIONAL RELATIONS
    Paul Wilkinson
MEMORY   Jonathan Foster
MODERN CHINA
    Rana Mitter
SCIENCE AND RELIGION
    Thomas Dixon
TYPOGRAPHY   Paul Luna

For more information visit our web site
www.oup.co.uk/general/vsi/

John Parker and Richard Rathbone

AFRICAN HISTORY

A Very Short Introduction

OXFORD
UNIVERSITY PRESS

OXFORD
UNIVERSITY PRESS

Great Clarendon Street, Oxford OX2 6DP

Oxford University Press is a department of the University of Oxford.
It furthers the University's objective of excellence in research, scholarship,
and education by publishing worldwide in

Oxford New York

Auckland Cape Town Dar es Salaam Hong Kong Karachi
Kuala Lumpur Madrid Melbourne Mexico City Nairobi
New Delhi Shanghai Taipei Toronto

With offices in

Argentina Austria Brazil Chile Czech Republic France Greece
Guatemala Hungary Italy Japan Poland Portugal Singapore
South Korea Switzerland Thailand Turkey Ukraine Vietnam

Oxford is a registered trade mark of Oxford University Press
in the UK and in certain other countries

Published in the United States
by Oxford University Press Inc., New York

British Library Cataloguing in Publication Data

Data available

Library of Congress Cataloging in Publication Data

Data available

Typeset by RefineCatch Ltd, Bungay, Suffolk
Printed in Great Britain by
Ashford Colour Press Ltd, Gosport, Hampshire

ISBN 978-0-19-280248-4

3 5 7 9 10 8 6 4

Contents

List of illustrations

The publisher and the authors apologize for any errors or omissions in the above list. If contacted they will be pleased to rectify these at the earliest opportunity.

List of maps

Chapter 1
The idea of Africa

This book is a very short introduction to a very big topic. In fact, it is a very short introduction to two very big topics. On the one hand, it is about a place and its people: Africa. On the other, it is about the past of that place, as it has been envisaged by Africans and written about by historians. The sheer scale of both place and past is colossal. Africa: an entire continent, in terms of language and culture the world's most diverse, stretching from the southern shores of the Mediterranean to the Cape of Good Hope and today comprising over 50 separate nations. The cradle of mankind, where humans first evolved and from where they fanned out to settle the earth, Africa also possesses a recoverable history stretching back five millennia to the earliest of the world's ancient civilizations, that of pharaonic Egypt.

To provide even the sparest chronological outline of this history as it unfolded across the diverse regions of the continent is way beyond my scope here. Besides, it would be as dry as the dust that each year the *harmattan* wind blows south from the Sahara desert, discolouring skies from Senegal to Sudan. There are already many volumes that provide overviews of African history, or of different parts of it. We recommend a selection of these at the end of the book. Rather, our aim is to reflect upon the changing ways that the African past has been imagined and represented. That said, we have not focused exclusively on history as the representation of the past to the exclusion of history as a sequence of actual events. Our arguments are illustrated by a range of events and processes dr. from across the continent, as well as from the African diaspora beyond its shores. From these examples, hopefully, will emerge some of the main issues, problems, and debates that have arisen from the study of the African past. These issues are critical not just for an understanding of Africa, but for an understanding of the entire discipline of history.

Neither is it simply the physical immensity of Africa coupled with the great depth and diversity of its past that makes our topic such a challenging one. It is also because the notion of 'African history' itself has been so controversial and contested: dismissed as unimportant by some, embraced as an ideological weapon by others, and all the time stubbornly resistant to precise definition. This last point may appear strange. Africa, as we have just stated, is a continent, and its past is what constitutes African history. But does a continent possess 'a history'? It is almost inconceivable that a book similar to this will be written on, say, 'Asian history' or 'European history'. Underlying the idea of a singular African history is the assumption that the continent possesses some kind of essential unity beyond the mere geographic, a unity that not only binds it together but that also sets it apart from other parts of the world.

Here, from the outset, the question of race enters the picture, because African history has often been seen as the history of black people. This raises a number of questions. Should African history be that of the entire continental landmass, encompassing the regions both north and south of the Sahara desert, and thereby including many peoples who are not demonstrably 'black'? Or is African history *essentially* that of sub-Saharan or 'black Africa'? If the latter, then should it encompass the tens of millions of Africans who have lived and died outside the continent, predominantly in the black diaspora created in the Americas and in Asia by the trade in slaves? Beyond the issue of inclusion and exclusion, there is a further question. Is African history in its essence the same as that of other peoples or parts of the world, subject to the same 'universal truths' and amenable to the same methods of scholarly analysis? Or does the particularity of Africa demand that its past be studied according to its own logic, or even to the diverse logics of its myriad constituent parts? How 'African', in other words, is African history?

Historians from both inside and outside the continent continue to debate these issues. Again, this may seem surprising. What does it say about the study of African history that scholars are divided over such fundamental definitions? A partial answer to this question lies in the fact that although African history is a huge topic, it is also a very new one. As a recognized academic endeavour, it has emerged only in the last four or five decades. In the 19th and the first half of the 20th century, as the modern discipline of history became established in Western universities, the general European perception was that Africa, especially sub-Saharan Africa, had no history to speak of. Not only were its societies regarded as primitive and unchanging, they were believed, due in large part to the widespread absence of literacy, to possess no collective historical consciousness.

These racial perceptions were part and parcel of the era of European imperialism and were mobilized to justify the conquest and partition of Africa at the end of the 19th century. Despite the collapse of pseudo-scientific racial hierarchies and of colonial empires in the aftermath of the Second World War, doubts over the validity of an African history continued to be voiced into the second half of the 20th century – including, notoriously, by some leading (European) members of the history profession. The doubters were wrong about the absence of historical consciousness. African peoples have long had their *own* perceptions of the past and their own ways of remembering it. African history is not simply something that is 'done' in modern universities. But the recent acceptance of the African past as a legitimate part of the academic discipline – like that of other colonized peoples, of women, of the poor, of the hitherto voiceless and the marginalized generally – has been a crucial breakthrough in the recognition of the diversity of human history.

The invention of Africa

Before we begin to consider the contours of African history, we must first examine those of Africa itself. The two are not easily separated, because to think about Africa as a place, we must think historically. In recent decades, historians and other scholars, many of whom are increasingly suspicious of received wisdoms, have begun to scrutinize and to 'un-package' a range of political, social, and ideological entities that for a long time have simply been taken for granted. Some of this un-packaging has been directed towards the ways in which societies and individuals have seen themselves in the world, and has sought to demonstrate that such visions are more complex and more prone to change than has been assumed. It has also been concerned with the ways in which certain cultures have seen others, especially with how Europe or 'the West' has perceived the peoples of Asia, Africa, the Americas, and elsewhere. In addition to complexity and change, the emphasis here has been on how these perceptions say as much about the viewer as the viewed. They can also be seen to have been shaped by the dynamics of imperial power.

A groundbreaking work in this vein was Edward Said's *Orientalism* (1978), which examined the European vision of an exotic, decadent, and corrupted 'orient', including North Africa. Said has been much criticized for constructing in turn an inverted orientalism (or 'occidentalism') by assuming the existence of a monolithic European worldview. Yet his thesis, if flawed, has been influential, prompting a range of works reflecting on visions of the world with titles such as *Imagining India*, by Ronald Inden, and *The Invention of Africa*, by the Congolese philosopher V. Y. Mudimbe. How was Africa invented? And by whom? The short answer, according to Mudimbe, is that the idea of Africa was initially fashioned not by ans but by non-Africans, as a 'paradigm of difference'. Africa, [in ot]her words, has served as an exotic prism through which [out]siders, mainly Europeans, refracted images of 'the other' and of [t]hemselves.

There is much evidence to support this view. Before the 20th century, very few of Africa's inhabitants thought of themselves as 'Africans'. The origin of the word itself can be traced back to the nexus of classical civilizations in the ancient Mediterranean. It was the Greeks who first envisaged a three-way division of the Mediterranean world, calling its southern shores Libya as opposed to Asia to the east and Europa to the northwest. Between Libya and Asia lay 'Egypt' (another Greek word), whose great river, the Nile, was seen by ancient geographers as dividing the two realms.

For the Greeks, the term 'Libyans' (*Libyes*) seems to have had a vague racial connotation, as it was used to distinguish the peoples of the Mediterranean coast from darker-skinned 'Ethiopians' (from *Aithiops*, lit. 'burnt-faced') to the south. Greek observers divided the Libyans into numerous 'tribes', one of which, that around the Phoenician outpost of Carthage (in modern Tunisia), later Roman sources refer to as the Afri. Africa, 'the land of the Afri', was originally applied in a strictly limited sense to the Roman province created after the conquest of Carthage in 146 BC. Following the demise of the Roman empire and the Arab conquest of North Africa in the 7th century AD, the same coastal region became known, in Arabic, as 'Ifriqiya'. But it was only from the 15th century, when Portuguese mariners brought the outline of Africa into the purview of Europe, that the term was generally applied to the entire continent.

The Portuguese voyages of the 'age of discovery' not only served to expand European knowledge of Africa, they also initiated a process that would transform European thinking about Africans. The context for this transformation was the transatlantic slave

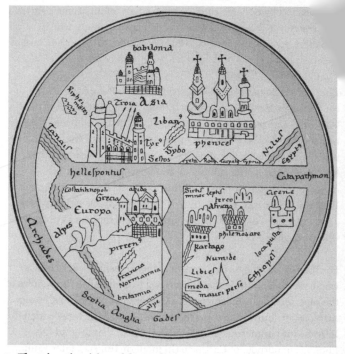

1. The tripartite vision of the Mediterranean-centred world. A so-called medieval 'T map', from an 11th-century Leipzig codex, with the Nile river indicated on the frontier of Asia; Carthage, Numidia, Libya, and 'Mauri' in North Africa; and, at the outer extremities of the known world, 'Ethiopia', 'Scotia', and 'Anglia'

trade. Slavery had been a prominent feature of the classical Mediterranean world and had continued in various forms in medieval Europe. It also existed in the Muslim world, including North Africa, and in sub-Saharan Africa itself. Yet it was the Atlantic slave trade, which between the 16th and the 19th centuries involved the forced migration of some 12 million Africans to the Americas, that forged an explicit link in European minds between racial inferiority, enslavement, and Africa. We will return to slavery and the slave trade in Chapter 4. The point to be noted here is that the modern idea of Africa emerged, in many ways, from the dehumanizing crucible of Atlantic slavery.

It was from that crucible, moreover, that Africans themselves first began to appropriate the idea of Africa. The first to do so were Western-educated intellectuals from the black diaspora, men like the celebrated anti-slave trade campaigner Olaudah Equiano and 19th-century African Americans like Alexander Crummell, Martin Delany, and Edward W. Blyden. Able to perceive Africa because of their very removal from it, these thinkers laid the foundations of what came to be known as 'pan-Africanism'. They did so by appropriating not just the idea of Africa, but also the 19th-century European language of race. In early pan-Africanist thought, Africa – or 'Ethiopia', as the continent continued sometimes to be called – was seen as the home of a distinctive people, the 'Negro race'. It was only towards the end of the 19th century that these ideas began to develop within Africa itself, emerging first among the literate, English-speaking communities of the trading towns of coastal West Africa. By then, the continent stood on the cusp of European colonial conquest, a condition that would further consolidate for many what it meant to be African.

The idea of Europe, as recent research on the Middle Ages shows, was as much an act of imagination as that of Africa. Neither were Europeans the only outsiders to 'discover' the continent. The others were Muslim Arabs, who in the seven decades following the death of the Prophet Muhammad in 632 AD swept out of the Arabian peninsula, conquering the whole of coastal North Africa, and in 711 extending their rule over Spain and Portugal. North Africa, which in Roman times had been an early centre of Christianity, became predominantly Muslim. The majority of its indigenous Egyptian and Berber peoples converted to Islam, mixing with the influx of Arab migrants to create distinctively North African cultures and political dynasties. Muslim geographers to some extent inherited the tripartite division of the known world from Greek thought, but this was overlaid with a more fundamental worldview based on faith. Thus, North Africa became an integral part of the *Dar al-Islam*, the abode of Islam, while the region across the Sahara desert to the south lay in the *Dar al-Kufr*, the abode of unbelief, sometimes called the *Dar al-Harb*, the realm of war.

By the end of the first millennium, camel-riding Berber and Arab traders had begun to forge links across the Sahara with what they called the *bilad as-Sudan*, 'the lands of the blacks'. With trade came Islam itself, attracting converts from amongst the commercial and the ruling elites of West Africa's savanna kingdoms and serving to blur the Muslim distinction between the realms of belief and unbelief. A similar process was underway on Africa's eastern coast, which became connected into Muslim networks of maritime trade in the Indian Ocean. Like later Atlantic commerce, trans-Saharan and Indian Ocean trade also included the export of slaves, although for Muslims it was 'paganism' rather than skin colour that remained the principal justification for enslavement. Yet medieval Arabic writing on the *bilad as-Sudan*, even that by sophisticated thinkers such as the famous North African historian Ibn Khaldun, often expresses a disdain for 'primitive' Africans that goes beyond their status as pagans. For Muslim North Africans too, black Africa was conceived as a 'paradigm of difference'.

North Africa has in turn presented a problem for those who have sought to define Africa and the 'black race'. Europeans in the age of imperialism may have perceived the region as part of a decaying orient, as Said argues. But it was still seen to lie within the realm of history – in contrast with the timeless primitiveness of 'tribal' Africa to the south. Amongst 19th-century pan-Africanists – most of whom believed that Africa's 'redemption' would come through conversion to Christianity – the issue often turned on differing attitudes towards Islam. Some, such as Blyden, had a highly favourable view of the religion; others regarded it as part of the problem, due to some extent to its ongoing association with slavery. Victorian racial myths also gave rise to the 'Hamitic hypothesis' (from the biblical Ham, the son of Noah): the notion

-skinned invaders from the north were responsible for the
on of whatever cultural achievement was deemed to exist
ack Africa. This theory too was assimilated by many early
n-Africanists, anxious to draw black people into the universal
story from which they had been barred by establishing a link
between African culture and the Middle Eastern origins of
Christianity.

The 19th-century notion that humankind can be divided into
discrete races has now been abandoned by geneticists and
historians alike. So too, by and large, have grand theories suggesting
the diffusion of some kind of essentialized 'African civilization'. The
problem of defining Africa, however, persists, as is suggested by a
comparison of recent textbooks by two of the continent's leading
historians. John Iliffe's *Africans: The History of a Continent*, as its
subtitle indicates, treats African history as that of the entire
continent, north and south of the Sahara. Frederick Cooper's *Africa
since 1940*, in contrast, ignores North Africa, limiting its scope to
the sub-Saharan region, and by doing so implying that it is the latter
that represents what is distinctive about African history. At the
other end of the continent, South Africa, with its history of white
settlement and industrialization, also sits uncomfortably in many
textbooks: Iliffe consigns its modern history to a self-contained
chapter at the end of his work. Both books, as is conventional,
include the huge Indian Ocean island of Madagascar as part of
Africa -- although both, as is also conventional, have very little to
say about it.

Other scholars argue for the inclusion of the diaspora, insisting that
African history, far from stopping neatly at the edge of the
continent, reaches out into what has been called the 'black Atlantic'.
None of these approaches are right or wrong. We have already
noted the importance of the diaspora in the formulation of the idea
of Africa, and will return later to debates over its broader role in the
African past. With regard to North Africa, culturally, historically,
and even geographically, the region can be seen to be as much a part

of the Mediterranean world, of southwest Asia, or of the Mic
East as it is a part of Africa. Yet it is, we would argue, *at least*
'Races', 'tribes', 'kinship systems', and a variety of other framewe
into which outside observers have squeezed African societies hav
now been abandoned or questioned. But too much progress has
been made since the 1950s in the recovery of the continent's past to
abandon the idea of Africa itself.

The lie of the land: environment and history

'Africa' may well be an invented idea. But it is also a physical reality:
a diverse range of environments and landscapes that have formed
the context for its human history. Environmental history has been
very much in vogue in recent years. Its prominence is due in part to
escalating concerns about global climate change, population
growth, famine, and ecological crisis. John Iliffe's *Africans*,
published in 1995, takes as its organizing theme the continent's
demographic history, placing great emphasis on the role of Africans
as the 'frontiersmen who have colonized an especially hostile region
of the world on behalf of the entire human race'. The building of
enduring societies in a harsh environment of 'ancient rocks, poor
soils, fickle rainfall, abundant insects, and unique prevalence of
disease', Iliffe argues, represents a triumph against adversity.
Yet that triumph has been hard-won, for it has come at a cost of
great human suffering and of Africa's ongoing poverty. 'It is
time for understanding', he insists, 'for reflection on the place
of contemporary problems in the continent's long history'.

That our perceptions of the past are determined by the concerns of
the present is a common and even clichéd observation. Famously,
Edward Gibbon's *Decline and Fall of the Roman Empire*, one of
the foundation stones of modern history writing, has been
interpreted as reflecting late 18th-century anxieties about the
decline of the British empire. Perhaps. But there is no doubt that
the field of African history has been influenced by the fluctuating
fortunes of the continent over the last 50 years. Inspired by the

tion struggles against colonial rule and by the building of
 ependent nations, the pioneering generation of historians in the
 Os tended to focus their attention on political history –
 pecially that of indigenous African states. In the 1970s, as
 olitical turmoil and economic decline became the order of the
day, economic history came to the fore. This in turn was succeeded
by a growing interest in social history, that is, the lived experience
of ordinary people rather than a narrow focus on the actions of
'great men'.

We will return at various points to this trajectory, including the
most recent 'turn' towards cultural and intellectual history. The
historiography of Africa has, of course, been more complex than
that: more a set of overlapping and contested perspectives than
the linear evolution outlined here. Yet it reminds us that ways of
thinking about Africa continue to evolve. And this goes for
something as apparently solid as the physical environment
itself. As James McCann writes in a recent survey of the topic,
'environmental and landscape history is also, to a large degree,
the history of ideas, perceptions, and prescriptions about what
historical African cultures and colonial governments felt about
how land should look'. We haven't yet finished, in other words,
with invented or imagined ideas about Africa.

How, then, does Africa look? In terms of topography, it is less
extreme than other continents. Mountainous regions do exist:
mainly the Atlas mountains of Morocco and Algeria, and the spine
of highlands running from Eritrea south through the Rift Valley, the
Great Lakes region, and on to the Drakensberg in South Africa.
Famously, Mount Kilimanjaro's snow-capped summit rises 5,895
metres above the equator – although in these times of global
warming its white cap is visibly retreating. But only 4% of the
continent lies above 1,500 metres, and half of that is in the
Abyssinian highlands of Ethiopia and Eritrea. The core of the
continent is a massive plateau of ancient rocks, elevated towards the
east but dominated by a series of vast alluvial flatlands. Like Africa's

rocks, its soils are ancient – and many, for the purposes of agriculture, are very poor.

Outside its more fragmented eastern highlands, Africa's ecology changes dramatically in a sequence of lateral bands as rainfall level decline either side of the equator. Northwards, the equatorial rainforest of the Congo basin and the West African coast gives way to woodland and then savanna grassland, which in turn are succeeded by the semi-arid Sahel, the vast expanse of the Sahara desert, and finally the wetter Mediterranean littoral of North Africa. South of the equator, the pattern is repeated, with savanna giving way in the west to the Kalahari and Namib deserts and then the temperate climate of South Africa's Cape.

Many of these ecological zones have indeed proved tough-going for human habitation. Challenging terrains, extreme climates, and high levels of disease all contributed to Africa's historically low population levels. Scattered, mobile populations in turn limited the ability of would-be state-builders to establish centralized political power. But few historians these days would argue that the environment actually *determined* the course of human events. This was not always the case. Indeed, 'environmental determinism' was central to European perceptions of Africa in the imperial age – as it was to older Muslim perceptions of the tropics. That is, racial characteristics were widely believed to have arisen from environmental conditions, with the 'enervating' tropical climate being a root cause of black African backwardness.

And no milieu was deemed to be more enervating than the equatorial forest. Primeval, impenetrable, monotonous, and, above all, dark, 'the jungle' was seen to have bred the most extreme primitiveness. It was – and in many ways remains – the most persistent popular myth about the African landscape. As a metaphor for African 'otherness', it is present from Victorian travel literature to Joseph Conrad's famous novella *Heart of Darkness* (1901), Duke Ellington's 'jungle music' of the 1920s, and on to

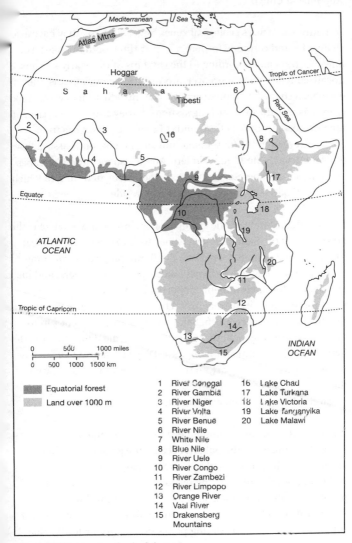

Map 1. Africa: main physical features

1	River Senegal	16	Lake Chad
2	River Gambia	17	Lake Turkana
3	River Niger	18	Lake Victoria
4	River Volta	19	Lake Tanganyika
5	River Benue	20	Lake Malawi
6	River Nile		
7	White Nile		
8	Blue Nile		
9	River Uele		
10	River Congo		
11	River Zambezi		
12	River Limpopo		
13	Orange River		
14	Vaal River		
15	Drakensberg Mountains		

Equatorial forest

Land over 1000 m

contemporary reportage of political violence in the Democratic Republic of Congo.

Not only are Africa's ecological zones hugely diverse, they have also changed – and continue to change – over time, both in long-term linear fashion and according to the rhythms of the yearly seasons. Localized landscapes, moreover, are 'anthropogenic', that is, they have been shaped by human action. The introduction of exotic food crops has transformed farming systems: barley and wheat arrived in the northeast from Asia thousands of years ago, bananas from Southeast Asia in the first millennium, and maize and cassava from the Americas in the 1500s. Modern Africa also includes cityscapes constructed of concrete, glass, wood, and corrugated iron, in which nearly half of the continent's people now reside.

Perhaps the most dramatic example of environmental change is the drying out of the Sahara desert. About 10,000 years ago, tropical Africa's climate entered a period of high rainfall, which for some five millennia created a Saharan landscape of lakes, rivers, and lush grassland. This environment supported human habitation throughout much of the region. Archaeological evidence has shown that by the end of this epoch, Saharan populations had begun to move from hunting, fishing, and gathering to the domestication of livestock and the cultivation of grain. They also began to produce some of Africa's earliest art, in the form of striking rock paintings that can still be seen on the mountainous desert outcrops of the Adrar des Iforas in Mali, and Ahaggar and Tassili in Algeria.

About 5,000 years ago, rainfall began to decline and over succeeding millennia the Sahara became the great desert that we know today. The process of desiccation impacted in a variety of ways on human settlement, pushing pastoralist and agriculturalist peoples, together with their new food-producing techniques, southwards into East Africa and into the forest fringes of the west. It forced others from the drying plains down into the fertile Nile Valley, creating a concentration of population that facilitated the

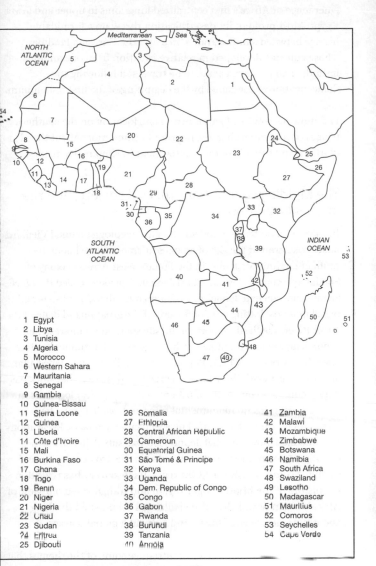

1 Egypt	26 Somalia	41 Zambia
2 Libya	27 Ethiopia	42 Malawi
3 Tunisia	28 Central African Republic	43 Mozambique
4 Algeria	29 Cameroun	44 Zimbabwe
5 Morocco	30 Equatorial Guinea	45 Botswana
6 Western Sahara	31 São Tomé & Principe	46 Namibia
7 Mauritania	32 Kenya	47 South Africa
8 Senegal	33 Uganda	48 Swaziland
9 Gambia	34 Dem. Republic of Congo	49 Lesotho
10 Guinea-Bissau	35 Congo	50 Madagascar
11 Sierra Leone	36 Gabon	51 Mauritius
12 Guinea	37 Rwanda	52 Comoros
13 Liberia	38 Burundi	53 Seychelles
14 Côte d'Ivoire	39 Tanzania	54 Cape Verde
15 Mali	40 Angola	
16 Burkina Faso		
17 Ghana		
18 Togo		
19 Benin		
20 Niger		
21 Nigeria		
22 Chad		
23 Sudan		
24 Eritrea		
25 Djibouti		

Map 2. The present-day nation-states of Africa

emergence of Africa's first centralized kingdoms in upper and lower Egypt. Most profoundly, desertification threw up a formidable barrier between sub-Saharan Africa and the Eurasian landmass, whose cultures developed in relative isolation from one another until the Sahara began again to be traversed following the domestication of the camel by the beginning of the first millennium.

Let's now narrow our focus down to one location on the southern fringes of that desert barrier, in order to think more about the idea of Africa and the role of the environment in shaping its history.

The Middle Niger: urbanism, civil society, and the imperial tradition

In 1938, a schoolteacher and amateur archaeologist named Vieillard had a poke around the site of an old settlement three kilometres south of the town of Jenne, in the French West African colony of Soudan (present-day Mali). Local Jenneké-speakers called the place Jenne-jeno, 'ancient Jenne', one of numerous abandoned sites and burial mounds dotting the floodplains of the great inland delta of the Niger River. Vieillard's report on the site sparked no interest, and Jenne-jeno remained untouched by scholars and antiquity hunters alike. It was not until 1977, 17 years after Mali's independence, that archaeological work there began. Three decades later, that work has made Jenne-jeno one of the most important historical locations in Africa. It contains no monumental ruins and, aside from a few terracotta figurines, has yielded no spectacular artefacts. Excavations have revealed, however, that Jenne-jeno was sub-Saharan Africa's oldest yet known urban centre, founded in the 3rd century BC and occupied continuously for 1,600 years. Its discovery has rewritten the history of the Middle Niger region and transformed our view of Africa's urban past. It has also challenged established thinking about the emergence of towns and cities in a global context.

The story of Jenne-jeno serves to introduce some of the themes that we will develop in later chapters: the question of identities, the

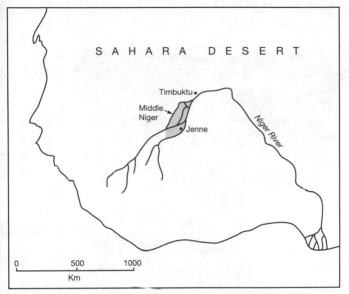

Map 3. The Middle Niger region of West Africa

problem of sources, and the tension between internal and external dynamics in African history. By extending the recoverable history of the Middle Niger back over 2,000 years, it also demonstrates the possibilities and the problems of applying to Africa the insights of the so-called *Annales* school of history pioneered in France in the first half of the 20th century: the importance of deep-rooted currents over the *longue durée* (the long term) and of *mentalité*, the distinctive 'mentality' of a particular time and place.

The middle reaches of the Niger River have long been central to perceptions of Africa. Lying within what Arabic-speakers called the Sahel (literally 'shore'), the arid southern fringe of the Sahara, it was associated with the succession of three empires that dominated the political landscape of the western Sudan from the 8th to the 16th century: Ghana, Mali, and Songhay. Ghana first enters the historical record at the end of the 8th century via the accounts of

17

2. Urban architecture as art form. A house in Jenne (in present-day Mali) in 1905: a fine example of the 'sudanic style' of mud-based architecture that stretches across the Sahel and savanna zones of West Africa. Photograph by Edmond Fortier (1862–1928), French West Africa's leading photographer and postcard publisher in the early colonial period. Based in Dakar in Senegal, Fortier produced some 3,300 images between 1900 and 1910

Muslim traders, drawn across the desert by the lucrative trade in gold controlled by its rulers. Six centuries later, it was this commerce that lured Portuguese mariners down the coast of Guinea. Trans-Saharan exchange and Islamic statecraft underpinned the process of sudanic empire-building, giving rise to Ghana's successors and to the entrepôt cities that emerged along the desert fringe: Jenne, to the south of the inland delta, and, to the north, the legendary Timbuktu.

That, at least, is the old-fashioned version of events. Even before the emergence of African history as an academic endeavour, the Ghana-Mali-Songhay sequence featured prominently in interpretations of the continent's past. For sympathetic colonial administrators, as well as for pioneering African American scholars, it was these great empires that most clearly emerged from the mists of time. For the first, so-called 'nationalist' generation of professional historians, too, it was states that were all-important. Their concern was to 'decolonize' the past by demonstrating that Africa, far from being the primitive tribal realm of European imperialist mythology, had a long and noble tradition of state-building. Nowhere was this more apparent than in the great sudanic empires such as Mali, which at its apogee during the reign of the famous Mansa Musa (1312–37) encompassed a vast domain and was renowned for its wealth and power throughout Europe and the Muslim world.

Recent archaeological research, combined with that by historians, art historians, and anthropologists, has forced a rethink of this established narrative. First, the excavation of Jenne-jeno shows that the emergence of towns in the Middle Niger occurred far earlier than indicated by oral traditions and Arabic chronicles. Far from being an isolated backwater, the region can now take its place as the last of the world's ancient urban civilizations to be discovered. Second, the lingering assumption that it was external forces that provided the catalyst for the development of 'complex societies' in sudanic West Africa has now conclusively been disproved. Well before the arrival of North African traders, Jenne-jeno was part of a

Naming nations

The appropriation of historic names by new nations can be confusing. Ironically, while the object was often to exorcize European colonial nomenclature and to establish a link with an authentic African past, some of these old names were coined by outside observers. Egypt, Libya, and Ethiopia are all originally Greek terms, while both Morocco and Mauritania (and the term 'Moors') are derived from the Roman word for one of the 'tribes' of North Africa. The British colony of the Gold Coast took the name Ghana at independence, although this was the Arabic name for a state that appears to have been called Wagadou by its own rulers (and which was thousands of miles from the Gold Coast in present-day Mali and Mauritania). With greater historical continuity, the French Soudan became Mali, while only the eastern part of the 'sudanic' zone (from *bilad as-Sudan*) retained the name Sudan. Perhaps the most striking renaming of a postcolonial African state took place when Haute Volta ('Upper Volta') combined words from two indigenous languages to become Burkina Faso, roughly translated as 'the land of the incorruptible man'.

flourishing regional network of trade. Third, the indigenous urban culture that did emerge took a very particular form. In short, the region's ancient urban landscape contains no traces of the monumental architecture that in other parts of the world point to the centralization of political power and of ritual authority. According to archaeologist Roderick McIntosh, the essence of Middle Niger civilization was not hierarchy but pluralist 'heterarchy'. Its real genius, in other words, may have been in the ability to organize itself *without* recourse to coercive state power, rather than in the glorious history of empire-building.

3. Terracotta figure of a mounted warrior excavated from a tumulus in the Jenne region, 13th–14th century: the imperial tradition personified. Cavalry technology was often crucial in the consolidation of centralized political power in the savannas of West Africa

The history of the Middle Niger over the *longue durée* has turned on the skilful management of a challenging physical environment and of an equally challenging human landscape. The former succeeded in sustaining what McIntosh describes as 'a vast alluvial garden abutting the bleak Sahara'. The latter secured social harmony through a process of 'ethnic accommodation', underpinned by a cluster of core symbolic values shared between the various peoples of the region: Soninke, Malinke, Bambara, and others. Prominent amongst these values were the autonomy of the local village community, or *kafu*, and notions of occult power, *nyama*. Over time they coalesced into what came to be known as Mande culture. Emerging from this deep reservoir of culture was what McIntosh calls the imperial tradition. It was a northern branch of the Mande cultural group, the Soninke, who dominated the kingdom of Ghana. From the Mande heartland to the south arose another branch, the Malinke, who in the 13th century eclipsed the remnants of Ghana's authority to establish a new system of overrule, that of Mali.

For the reconstruction of the imperial tradition, the historian can turn to other sources beyond the archaeological record: the accounts of North African travellers and geographers, locally written Arabic chronicles (*ta'rikh*), and the *kuma koro* or 'ancient speech' of the Mande themselves. Towards the end of the first millennium AD, in other words, prehistory begins to shade into history. Compared to the wealth of written records produced in medieval Europe, or in India or China in the same period, however, such sources are few and fragmented. Those that do exist, moreover, present the historian with problems of interpretation. Over-reliance on the views of Muslim visitors and chroniclers, for example, in part explains the early emphasis on the role of external factors (notably, trans-Saharan trade and Islam) in the emergence of states. The use of indigenous oral traditions has helped to redress the balance – but these too are problematic, most being recorded for the first time only in the 20th century. This is the case with the most famous repository of Mande *kuma koro*, the epic of Sunjata. An elaborate, Homeric song-cycle performed by a caste of bards called *jeliw* (or

Afrique Occidentale
1092. "Touareg", armés de lances, d'un sabre
dont le fourreau est fixé au poignet
gauche, et d'un bouclier

Collection générale Fortier, Dakar

4. Resistance to the imperial tradition. Tuareg horsemen armed with swords, lances, and shields and wearing their famous indigo-dyed robes and turbans, photographed by Edmond Fortier at Timbuktu in 1906. Tuareg confederations resisted the French conquest of the Sahara region for many decades (the figure in the centre may have been the chieftain who led an attack on the French military post at Timbuktu in 1913), and again rose in rebellion against the nation-state of Mali in the 1980s

griots), it tells the story of how Sunjata Keita overcame the Soso magician-king Sumanguru Kante and founded the empire of Mali.

After 1100 AD, Jenne-jeno went into decline, and by 1400 the town had been abandoned. The reasons are unclear, although the period was one of climatic instability and environmental stress – factors which also contributed to the unleashing of new forces and conflicts culminating in the rise of Mali. By the 15th century, Mali too was in decline, weakened by succession disputes, the infiltration of pastoralist nomads, and the rising power of its rival to the east, Songhay. As imperial overrule fragmented, local autonomies were reasserted. Society persevered, in other words, as states came and went.

Yet the imperial tradition was far from over. The apparent harmony of 'civil society' in the first millennium AD can be contrasted with the region's descent into violence and economic decline over the course of the last four centuries, as a succession of predatory state-builders struggled to impose their overbearing power on local communities. First came Moroccan conquerors, who crossed the desert to defeat Songhay in 1591, then the Bambara warrior-kings of Segou (17th century), the puritanical Islamic theocracy of Sekou Amadou (1818–62), the Tukulor empire of Umar Tal (1860s–90s), the French colonial state (1893–1960), and finally its postcolonial successor, the centralizing (and for many decades, military) regime of the Republic of Mali. Reconstructing this political narrative has been the easy part. Behind it lie more elusive histories of individual struggle and of social life that emerge only fleetingly onto the historical record. It is here that the challenge of recovering and representing African history lies.

Chapter 2
Africans: diversity and unity

We have emphasized the huge physical scale of the African
continent and we now turn to the even more intimidating variety of
the real focus of historical enquiry: Africa's peoples. Just as the idea
of Africa needs to be scrutinized carefully, so too does the idea of
'Africans'. Again, it seems obvious: Africa is a continent and the
people who live there are Africans. This simple, inclusive definition
is a good one. But again, it should not be taken for granted. As we
have seen, shifting perceptions of Africa, as well as scholarly debates
about the meanings of those perceptions, have actually been about
its people. When Muslim Arabs in the medieval period or
Europeans in the age of imperialism wrote of Africa as a 'primitive'
place without a history, what they were saying was that *Africans*
were primitive. Even today, historians are constantly confronted by
sweeping assertions about what 'Africans' do and think – including
what they might have done and thought in the past. Who are these
Africans? And how, historically, have they constructed their own
ideas of identity and belonging?

Diversity

Skeletal remains found in eastern Africa give every indication that it
was in this part of the world that human's hominid ancestors first
evolved, separating from the ancestors of chimpanzees between
four and six million years ago. We begin therefore with a simple

observation: that the history of mankind in Africa is older than that in any other continent. Part of the evidence for that time-depth is the sheer diversity of humanity to be found in Africa. Even the most casual visitor to any part of the continent today will rapidly recognize that generalizations about what Africans look like simply do not work. Africans are – and certainly always have been – variously tall and short, heavily built and slender, dark- and light-skinned, and so forth. While such visual impressions are imprecise, the scientific evidence shows that there is actually as much genetic variation within African populations than there is between Africans and Europeans. This immediately makes a nonsense of pseudo-scientific theories of racial difference, as well as challenging ideas about the distinct attributes of a singular 'African race'.

Yet physical attributes are a very small element of a much more interesting set of stories. To begin with, Africans speak a dizzying variety of languages. Due to the subtle differences between languages and dialects, the exact number is debatable, but a figure in the region of 1,500 is generally agreed upon by linguists. These have been divided into four broad, and sharply contrasting, families. Over 300 languages are spoken in Nigeria alone. We also know that many languages and dialects have been lost and are even now continuing to disappear, replaced by regional lingua francas such as Swahili, Hausa, and Lingala or by the continent's great languages of foreign import, Arabic, French, English, and Portuguese.

Beyond language, Africa's peoples historically have forged a multiplicity of cultures. 'Culture' can broadly be defined as the sum total of ideas, beliefs, values, and representations shared by the members of a given community. For a visitor to present-day Africa, or for a consumer of African culture outside the continent, this diversity is most apparent in the realm of representation, especially artistic expression: music, dance, the plastic arts, architecture, clothing, bodily decoration, and so on. Of these art forms, it is music that over the last century has been the most historically dynamic on a continental as well as a worldwide stage. The fusion in the Americas of African rhythm and European song transformed the world's popular music, giving rise to blues, jazz, samba, son, rock, soul, reggae, and rap. This musical revolution flowed from the diaspora back into the continent, where new popular styles emerged (and continue to emerge), ranging from rai in Algeria to West Africa's highlife, Congolese rumba, and South African township jazz.

Africans also believe in and – as they have been as questioning and contrary as anyone on the planet – have also harboured doubts about, a large number of religions. These range from innumerable examples of indigenous belief systems to those like Islam and Christianity, so-called world religions. The latter also come in a variety of forms, some of which constitute distinctive African contributions to the history of those beliefs. There are numerous examples of African innovation in the realm of world religions. Many of them, like the Muslim Murid brotherhood, whose origins lie in early 20th-century Senegal, or the Aladura churches of southwestern Nigeria, have now taken root in the cities of Europe and North America. So too have the continent's greatest spiritual exports, the *vodun* and *orisha*, West African deities who in Brazil and the Caribbean animated 'voodoo', santería, candomblé, and other hybrid religions. The ways in which extraordinarily large numbers of Africans have become Christian and Muslim – and the underlying resilience of indigenous beliefs are increasingly important themes in African historical studies

In the realm of political order, Africans have been members of a varied set of state forms. These have ranged from the most absolute kinds of monarchies to their polar opposites, societies whose absence of identifiable aristocracies or clear hierarchies of authority led anthropologists in the past to describe them as stateless or 'acephalous' (literally, headless). Travellers and other outsiders had little difficulty in coming to what they believed to be an understanding of Africa's kingdoms, as most of them had grown up

27

as subjects of emperors, kings, caliphs, or sultans. One need only read 19th-century European accounts of meetings with the powerful kings of Asante (in present-day Ghana) or of Buganda (in Uganda), for example, to catch this resonance. Meeting the *Asantehene*, British envoy Thomas Bowdich wrote from the Asante capital, Kumase, in May 1817, was 'indescribably imposing', the pomp and splendour serving to underline 'our impression of the power and influence of the monarch we are sent to conciliate'.

But when looking at societies in which rulers could not be identified, outsiders (as well as neighbouring Africans who presided over states) all too rapidly concluded that they were observing primitive anarchy rather than political order. In time, a more sustainable understanding emerged. Acephalous peoples were in fact subjected to authority, had laws, and were far from anarchic. While such societies differed from one another and changed over time, authority was usually vested in the representatives of their so-called 'segments' – families, clans, age groups, religious cults – usually senior men. Some observers have described such forms of government as comfortingly communal. But it is clear that they were not strangers to discriminatory gender division or other forms of social differentiation, and that order could be maintained by the use of coercion as well as negotiation. The notion that most Africans lived in harmonious village communities or were ruled over by benevolent kings before the violent imposition of European colonial rule is simply not borne out by the evidence. It does a disservice to the complexity of the continent's past.

Every region of Africa provides historians with examples of linguistic, cultural, and political diversity. These kaleidoscopic variations are both functions of, as well as actors in, historical processes. They did not just happen, nor have they been set in stone since time immemorial. They are the consequences of millennia of human movement, of conquest and subordination, of cultural exchange, of long-distance trade, of the dissemination of religious faiths, of colonialism and its demise – and of sexual attraction, which can transcend and then erode the barriers of perceived difference. Surveying this complex human tapestry, earlier historians of the continent were attracted by explanations that rested upon the large-scale physical movement of human populations, the idea of migration. Modern archaeological and linguistic research, however, seems more often to point to the gradual transmission of ideas, of languages, of cultures, and of technologies over space and time.

It will help to flesh some of this out by thinking about what being 'North African' might mean. Modern North Africans are descended from a rich *mélange* of indigenous Berber and Egyptian peoples, co-mingled with the inhabitants of ancient Greek, Phoenician, and Roman settlements, with Arab invaders, with long-resident Jewish communities, with returning 'Moors' from the Iberian peninsula, with sub-Saharan Africans drawn towards the Mediterranean by both enslavement and involvement in long-distance trade, and more recently with European settlers drawn not only from mainland France and Italy but also from culturally diverse islands such as Corsica, Malta, Sardinia, and Sicily. This constitutes a pretty distinguished heritage as well as a healthily constituted gene pool, the very converse of isolated 'in-breeding'.

But the history of genes tells us only so much. This diversity of origins also suggests the long gestation of distinctive cultures emerging from conflict as well as from mutual stimulation and borrowing. In art and architecture, in musical styles, in cooking, as well as in more heady intellectual or spiritual forms, there are clear indications of what we would today call 'fusion'. It requires no great expertise to hear echoes of medieval Andalucía, of the Sahel, and of Persia, for example, in the classical music of the Maghrib (that is, Morocco, Algeria, and Tunisia; in Arabic, 'the west'). Similarly, an enjoyable analysis of North African cuisine should lead to a realization of the mixing of the tastes of the southern shores of the Mediterranean with those to the north and the east: think of the

5. A *signar* (from the Portuguese *senhora*) or 'woman of colour of Senegal', from René de Villeneuve, *Afrique, ou histoire, moeurs, usages et coutumes des Africains* (Paris, 1814). Independent African or Euro-African merchants, *signares* exploited marital and commercial links with Europeans to accumulate wealth and influence on the island entrepôts of Gorée and Saint-Louis in the era of the slave trade

combination of dried fruits, olives, spices, and meat, for example, in the Moroccan *tagine*.

The North African example is admittedly an unusually rich one in global, let alone African, terms. But the histories of most African peoples can be interrogated in this fashion, despite the shortage of written evidence that often denies us texture as well as time-depth (see Chapter 3). Very few parts of Africa were untouched by the outside world, by neighbouring societies, or by much more distant 'others' before the colonial period. There were of course some exceptions: peoples whose physical remoteness made such contact less likely. But living in the depths of the equatorial rain forest, as did the 'pygmies' of the Ituri region of the present-day Democratic Republic of Congo, or in desert areas, like the San (or 'Bushmen') of the Kalahari in southern Africa, was seldom the result of accident. Isolation was frequently either the outcome of strategies devised by people unwilling to risk repeated predation by better-armed, hostile outsiders, or the consequence of being driven into marginal ecologies by more powerful peoples' capacity to confiscate richer arable land, pasture, or hunting grounds. Despite the 'new age' tendency to romanticize the San way of life, admittedly a brilliant adaptation to one of the harshest environments on the planet, most San would almost certainly have settled for a softer existence.

The scattered populations of Africans living such precarious hand-to-mouth lives using low levels of technology are not, as the romantics would have us believe, timeless 'stone age survivals'. Neither should those societies that did not develop hierarchical state systems be seen as somehow less 'advanced' than those which did. Colonial-era anthropologists often sought out isolated, stateless peoples in the belief that they constituted ideal laboratory specimens for understandings of how social systems evolved. But recent research has shown that Africa's many decentralized societies were as much the products of historical forces as its great kingdoms – including active resistance on the part of independent frontiersmen and -women to would-be state-builders. As we have seen with the Middle Niger, independent communities and cultures often persevered as predatory states rose and fell.

All of this should suggest that most, if not all, generalizations about Africans past and present are doomed to fail. Similarly, claims about whether this or that is 'authentic' or 'inauthentic', or whether individuals are 'full-blooded' or not, need to be understood for the ideological statements that they are. It makes no sense to be picky about those whom we should or should not consider to be the protagonists of African history. To repeat: historical Africans were the people who lived in Africa from the mouth of the Nile to the Cape of Good Hope, as well as on its outlying islands in the Atlantic and Indian Oceans. Recent historical study has also re-embraced their descendants, who through enslavement or voluntary migration have created communities beyond the shores of Africa, in the Americas and elsewhere (see Chapter 4). And finally, it must be remembered that Africans are men *and* women. Historical lives and experiences were profoundly shaped by this most fundamental of distinctions – a fact often overlooked by lazy generalizations about the past everywhere in the world.

A historian's definition of 'African' is necessarily broad and unracialized. If it includes, as it should, diasporic communities beyond Africa (including those that are no more, such as the Afro-European emirates of al-Andalus), then it must also extend to those peoples who have migrated *into* the continent and the hybrid societies that have emerged as a result. Such societies have long been characteristic of Africa's coastal littorals: from the complex *mélange* that is North Africa to the Swahili culture of East Africa, the Euro-African communities of the trading towns of the Atlantic coast, and on to the European, Malay, and Indian migrants drawn since the 17th century to South Africa. To reject the descendants of Dutch, French, English, and other 'white' settlers in southern Africa, or of Indians there and in East Africa, is arbitrary unless we are also prepared to reject those whose ancestors were part of the

6. White settlers. The commando of National Party supporters that escorted the late Dr Hendrik Verwoerd to the Party's 50th anniversary celebrations. The middle horseman in the front rank is Leon Wessels, who later became Deputy Minister of Law and Order in the National Party government. He was also the first senior member of that party to apologize for apartheid. De Wildt, Transvaal (North-Western Province), South Africa, October 1964. Photograph by David Goldblatt

extensive Omani diaspora in East Africa or of Arab expansion into North Africa.

Unity

Having said all that, it would be misleading to suggest that Africa is little more than a discordant hotchpotch of different peoples, cultures, and states. To emphasize difference alone runs the risk of falling back on an outmoded European vision of the continent as a jumble of unrelated, self-contained tribal groups – a vision that underpinned colonial conquest (on which more below). Indeed, historians are increasingly concerned to explore lines of 'interconnectedness', to move away from narrowly focused studies of particular ethnic groups, kingdoms, or nations in order to trace population movements, commercial linkages, and cultural flows over space and time. The search for such exchanges is now taking historical study beyond the edges of the continent itself, into the wider, diasporic arenas of the Atlantic, Indian Ocean, and Mediterranean worlds.

Just as importantly, to dismantle the notion of 'African-ness' is not to say that it has no intellectual purchase. Quite the opposite: the idea of a unitary people has been a key feature of the perceptions of outsiders and, over the last two centuries, of Africans. It has been especially prominent amongst a group that, in a way, was both: African Americans. As we have seen in Chapter 1, just as it was intellectuals in the diaspora who amongst Africans first began to perceive the contours of the entire continent, so was it they who appropriated from European thought the idea of a singular African people or, in the language of the time, a 'Negro race'. Whereas European and Anglo-American race theorists sought to denigrate black people, however, the pan-Africanist pioneers stressed racial unity as a tool of redemption.

To writings about racial unity, dignity, and redemption – what has been called 'vindicationist' literature – gradually were added layers

7. Arab settlers. Three officials of the Omani government of Zanzibar (part of present-day Tanzania), circa 1880s, whose status as members of the island's Arab aristocracy is marked by the wearing of a turban (in Swahili, *kilemba*) and the carrying of an ornamental dagger (*jambia*)

of historical speculation. By the end of the 19th century, a Hamitic
'counter-hypothesis' had begun to emerge, West Indian thinker
Edward W. Blyden suggesting that ancient Egypt was a Negro
civilization and the font of African culture. This found a curious,
inverted echo in the writings of the German ethnologist Leo
Frobenius, whose extensive travels through Europe's newly
conquered African colonies led to a theory of a residual ancient
civilization, remembered in European myth as the lost 'Atlantis'.
The first serious attempt at a continent-wide history, however, was
by the African American scholar and pan-African leader W. E. B.
Du Bois, whose *The Negro* (1915) provided a sweeping account
focused on racial unity and the glories of Africa's ancient kingdoms.
In 1922, *The Negro* became a key text in William Leo Hansberry's
history classes at Howard University in Washington, DC, the first
appearance of African history in a university curriculum.

Perhaps the most striking inversion of European conceptions of
Africa was that of *négritude*. A literary movement founded in Paris
in the 1930s by French-speaking African and West Indian
intellectuals, *négritude* sought to refute the imperialist racial divide
between civilized Europe and primitive Africa by demonstrating the
latter's rich cultural heritage. In doing so, however, it clung to the
idea of difference, emphasizing the particular attributes of a
homogenous 'African people'. In this respect, *négritude* can be
contrasted with the finer-grained historical and ethnographic
writings of earlier anglophone West African scholars such as the
Rev. Samuel Johnson, who tended to focus on their own peoples.
Parochial perhaps, but Johnson for one had no truck with
essentialized racial difference, stressing instead the striking cultural
similarities between the Yoruba and the British.

The demise of pseudo-scientific race theory in the second half of the
20th century, together with the application of the evidential rules of
the discipline of history to the study of the African past, have not
ended the appeal of the idea of a singular African civilization. It has
survived to the present in the form of various diffusionist-type

8. Black settlers. E. J. Roye (1815-72). Born in Newark, Ohio, Roye migrated to Liberia in 1846, made a fortune as a trader, and was elected president in 1869, serving for two years before being deposed in 1871. Founded in 1821 and becoming an independent republic in 1847, the African American settler colony of Liberia was an important symbol for 'vindicationist' thinking about Africa and the black race. Roye's pose appears to echo that depicted in a famous photograph of US president Abraham Lincoln

theories, some of which pose as works of historical research but which in fact represent little advance on the musings of Blyden and Frobenius. This type of writing has been called 'Afrocentrism'. A more accurate term, however, might be Egyptocentrism, as much of it remains transfixed by the notion that pharaonic Egypt was the font of all African culture and/or a distinctively 'black' civilization. Not all of this genre is devoid of scholarship: Martin Bernal's well known *Black Athena* (1987), for example, represents a serious attempt to engage with the history of cross-cultural exchange in the ancient eastern Mediterranean. But most of it is wild polemic, and all of it is deeply flawed on empirical grounds. It remains marginal to the mainstream academic study of African history. 'African unity' remains a powerful *ideological* construct, the evolution of which demands serious study. Ideology, however, can not replace history – and the unfolding history of Africa's peoples has been a lot more complex than Afrocentric theory allows.

Identity

For historians of Africa, no less than for Africans past and present, identity can be a tricky intellectual issue. Africans are, like people everywhere, compilations of numerous identities, some of which are personally or collectively claimed, others of which are imposed by outsiders. If people are asked who the most famous living African is, the usual answer is 'Nelson Mandela'. But as we write this in the aftermath of the 2006 World Cup, there is a good case for saying that the most famous living African is Zinédene Zidane. Let's consider this one individual. Who, or what, is Zidane? He's a Frenchman, born and raised in Marseilles. But he's also a North African, whose parents emigrated from Algeria; and a Berber, with family roots in the Kabyle mountains and reportedly fiercely proud of his ancestral village. He also describes himself as a (non-practising) Muslim. And he is, of course, a footballer. Whichever of these labels Zidane himself chooses to use would depend both on where he is and how he's thinking at the time. Identity, in other words, is as fluid as it is multifaceted.

But that is the easy part. Identities, even family identities, are often not as straightforward as they seem. Along with the rest of humanity, Africans are biologically members of immediate families and of wider networks of kin. 'Kinship' was a staple concern of colonial-era anthropologists, who learned that Africans had been unusually creative in devising ways of managing family affairs. Indeed, almost every type of kinship system can be illustrated with an African example. Unlike other kinds of human categorization, these kinds of affinity can ultimately be proved or disproved by modern methods of genetic enquiry. After all, you either are your great-grandmothers' great-grandchild, or you are not.

Yet most claims about kinship are not yet subjected to genetic testing. In Africa, as in other parts of the world, that has created space for imagination and invention. Historically, many individuals or families claimed relationships with others who were more aristocratic, wealthy, or spiritually influential. Some such claims were based upon genuine descent, but others were fictional. The ability of groups to maintain such fictions over time owed everything to their power, to their collective capacity to silence those who could cast doubt on such claims. Similarly, groups and individuals with legitimate claims to birth-derived advantage had those claims set aside if they lacked enough power to sustain them.

Other kinds of identity – racial, political, cultural, religious – are no more straightforward and no less political and debatable. And they are sometimes potentially very dangerous: millions of people in the 20th century alone have been killed because of their identification by others. Africa has provided us with an example in the genocide in Rwanda in 1994, when people deemed to be 'Tutsi' by extremists within the 'Hutu' majority were systematically hunted down and killed. In the space of a single month, an estimated 800,000 people – both Tutsis and moderate Hutus identified as sympathizers by the killers – lost their lives. We shall return to the history of this tragedy below.

Historians therefore endlessly interrogate such labels and identifications. But they are obliged to be every bit as inquiring about Africans' own identities, the identities they claim for themselves, as they are about those which have been foisted upon them by others. The scholarly consensus today regards non-biological identities as being, in one way or another, the product of historical processes. They are, in other words, 'constructed' by human agency, whether deliberately or inadvertently. And once constructed, identities are rarely static; they can be altered. Circumstances can force or encourage people to change their identities. Let's look at two examples from Africa's volatile 19th century, a time of tumultuous change throughout much of the continent.

The first is the forging of Zulu identity in southern Africa. This involved state-building, military conquest, physical expansion, the absorption of refugees and defeated people, and, ultimately, defeat and colonization at the hands of the British empire. Consequently, the meaning of being Zulu shifted over time, just as those claiming to be or being identified as Zulu constituted a rapidly changing population. Before about 1820, the word 'Zulu' connoted a clan name, that of the rulers of a small kingdom dominated by the larger and more powerful Mthetwa kingdom. Military innovation and the strategic genius of the Zulu ruler, Shaka, eventually allowed the small Zulu kingdom to overcome their Mthetwa overlords and in time to defeat a large number of other kingdoms in the region, some of which came to regard themselves as Zulu. This identity was fundamentally political, as there were other kingdoms in the wider region that were not so incorporated but which shared many cultural attributes, including language, with the Zulu.

For our second example we turn to the Yoruba people of present-day southwestern Nigeria and the neighbouring Republic of Bénin. Like the term 'Zulu', 'Yoruba' meant something quite different by the early 20th century than it had done a hundred years before. In fact, it was originally a word used by the Hausa people from the

9. Shaka (d. 1828). A famous engraving of the Zulu state-builder, based on a drawing by the English trader James King, from Nathaniel Isaacs, *Travels and Adventures in Eastern Africa* (London, 1836)

savanna to the north to describe the inhabitants of Oyo, just one of the many city-states into which the region was divided. Despite underlying affinities of language and culture, it was these city-based kingdoms that provided the focus of political and ethnic identity. When in the early 19th century the most powerful, Oyo, went into decline in the face of attacks from Hausa and Fulani Muslim revolutionaries, the region descended into decades of internecine warfare. It was a time of turmoil. Refugees were on the move, new towns were founded, and large numbers of captives were sold down to European slave traders on the coast. Many ended up as slaves in Brazil and Cuba. Others, intercepted at sea by the anti-slave trade squadron of the Royal Navy, were liberated thousands of miles away at the coastal colony of Sierra Leone. And it was here that the idea of being 'Yoruba' began to be reformulated.

The key actors in this process were Western-educated, literate Christians, men like Samuel Ajayi Crowther (c. 1806–91), liberated from a Portuguese slaver in 1822 and ordained as an Anglican pastor in 1843. That year, he published his *Grammar and Vocabulary of the Yoruba Language* in London, and the following year led the first Yoruba-language church service in Freetown, Sierra Leone. In 1845, Crowther returned home as an agent of the Church Missionary Society, joining other returning Sierra Leonians as well as freed slaves from Brazil (where ideas about Yoruba-ness had also been evolving) in an effort to create a modern, reinvigorated Yorubaland. Although both groups included Muslims, it was Christianity that lay at the heart of this project to forge a new, expanded sense of community. Another Sierra Leonian pastor, Samuel Johnson, even argued in his famous *History of the Yorubas* (1921, but completed 1897) that the rulers of Oyo – his own ancestors – were actually descended from Old Testament figures and that their religion had once been monotheistic. Conversion to Christianity, therefore, represented a *return* to ancient Yoruba ideals, which had been corrupted by 'heathenism', political fragmentation, and the slave trade. Through it lay the path to a modern Yoruba nation.

The Zulu and Yoruba are just two examples of the many African peoples who undertook what can be called projects of 'ethnogenesis' over the last few centuries. The key word here is 'projects': that is, these were conscious attempts – in our examples, by a militarized aristocracy and a Christianized elite – to revamp and to expand ideas of belonging. Both, of course, were more complex than described here. Within the evolving realms of Zulu-ness and of Yoruba-ness, as well as beyond them, there was much debate over the exact content and the meanings of these labels. They were further complicated, moreover, by both putative 'nations' being subsumed into broader political identities following colonial conquest. Individually and collectively, new boundaries needed to be worked out: between being Zulu and South African, Yoruba and Nigerian, and between being South African or Nigerian and 'African'. This working out continued down the generations and, for many, continues today.

'Tribes'

As we write, a popular documentary programme has just ended its second series on BBC television. It follows the experiences of its presenter, Bruce Parry, who each week immerses himself with much gusto in the culture of a different African people living in Ethiopia's Omo river valley. The name of the series is *Tribe*. It's interesting and sometimes enlightening – but there is a problem. Much misunderstanding of the question of identity in Africa is the consequence of centuries-old perceptions of Africans by others. European travellers, missionaries, colonial administrators, and ethnographers in the past have tended to collapse multiple identities into the single concept of 'tribe'. This was an outsiders' model of who Africans were and how they lived. It carried various loaded meanings for those who used it, often saying as much about them as it did about the reality of African states and societies.

One problem with the concept is its implicit idea that there is a close fit between the multiple identities we all have and the political states to whose rule we are subjected. This implied that people who were the subjects of, for example, the Asante or the Ethiopian *state* – political identities – were also necessarily linked to one another by other identities derived from kinship, religion, culture, or language. In reality, most African state-builders ruled over plural populations that seldom displayed the neat conformities assumed by the idea of 'tribe'. While there were states in which a relatively high proportion of the population were linked by blood, culture, and religious inclination, recent historiography has emphasized the physical mobility of Africans and the dynamism of material, intellectual, and social experimentation.

We are also continually confronted with assertions about the divisive, unbridgeable quality of 'tribal' membership. Returning to the example of the Hutu and the Tutsi in Rwanda and neighbouring Burundi might be instructive. There was a widespread belief in the world's press that the animosity that led to genocide in Rwanda in 1994 was based upon some primeval tribal distinction. The Tutsi, we were told, were tall pastoralists who traditionally dominated the shorter Hutu, who were arable farmers. The Tutsi were regarded by Rwanda and Burundi's European colonizers, first Germans and then, after the First World War, Belgians, as exemplifying the Hamitic ideal. That is to say, they were believed to be aristocratic invaders from the north who had conquered the indigenous, Bantu-speaking Hutu.

There is a lot of history to unpick here. The simplistic tribal model simply does not work. From what we know about the region before the advent of colonialism, political power had for centuries been contested between a scatter of kingdoms, but the fault lines of these conflicts were not related to a division between Tutsi and Hutu. The relationship between these two groups was much more complicated. To begin with, the Tutsi and the Hutu speak the same language, Banyarwanda. Moreover, plenty of Hutu were cattle-keepers before and during the colonial period; there were also dominant Hutu and subservient Tutsi in the precolonial period. And Hutu could and did become Tutsi, just as Tutsi became Hutu. While the meanings of 'Hutu' and 'Tutsi' have changed dramatically over time, such meanings were almost certainly derived from dynamic, shifting distinctions between groups with access to royal power. And the volatility of those identities was one of the consequences of change as well as being one of the authors of change.

The idea of 'tribe' is connected with the language of empires. It was the way in which Roman conquerors envisaged the indigenous Berber peoples of North Africa (the word 'Berber' originates from the Greek *barbaroi*, 'barbarians'), as well as wild and unruly Britons, Gauls, and Germans. Some have suggested that 'tribe' has not always had such pejorative connotations. After all, this is the way in which the King James Bible describes the divisions of the 'Children of Israel'. Yet the modern use of the term was forged in the crucible of European imperial expansion. By the late 19th century, European politicians were confident that they had created the highest form of social organization known to history, the nation-state. This, they believed, was a rational, modern construct, an alternative to older, undemocratic empires and kingdoms. The use of the word 'tribe' to describe African societies emerged from a desire to commend the nation-state while suggesting the inherent inferiority of others. It also served as a moral justification for colonial conquest. In one short, simple word, it connoted primitive polities that were less developed than nation states, cultures that had yet to be illuminated by the insights of the Enlightenment, technologies untouched by modern science, and religions that were superstitious rather than spiritual.

Matters were not to rest there. In time, colonial rule in many parts of Africa was to co-opt the services of the precolonial polities whose sovereignty had been usurped by conquest. It sought to use the rulers of older African states as auxiliaries in the tasks of keeping the peace, taxing the population, building roads, and mobilizing labour. Such devolved systems of local government were based on what were sanctified as tribal areas. Sometimes such areas corresponded to the scope of precolonial jurisdictions. Often they did not. In areas where there were no discernible kingdoms – or 'chiefdoms' as colonial rulers preferred to call them – Africans were encouraged to generate chiefs. In southeastern Nigeria, for example, so-called 'warrant chiefs' were created in acephalous Igbo-speaking areas whose legitimacy rested on warrants issued by the British regime. In many areas, chiefs lacked traditional legitimacy but had done the colonial state some service in the army or the police.

In many cases, new identities were invented or old ones re-imagined by a combination of colonial intervention and indigenous agency. Lee Cronk's study of the Mukogodo people of Kenya shows how this group of hunting-gathering (and bee-keeping) people came in the course of the first half of the 20th century to abandon their self-identity as Mukogodo in favour of identifying themselves as Maasai. The catalyst in this process was the reservation by the British colonial state of some of the most fertile lands of highland Kenya for the use of white settlers. The Mukogodo were decreed to be the original inhabitants of part of the land and were allocated a reserve of their own, which they used to expand from a foraging to a pastoral economy. The neighbouring Maasai had long regarded cattle-keeping as a superior way of life: in Maa the foraging life was insultingly called *il-torrobo*. But the British mistakenly understood the pejorative term *il-torrobo* to be a tribal name, the Dorobo. 'The Dorobo' themselves, however, had other ideas. Now lording it over their neighbours by building up cattle stocks on their own reserved land, they had gone up in the world. They were in the process of becoming Maasai.

This shift was not a slight matter in either emotional or intellectual terms for those making it. It involved the discarding of an older identity, partly configured around the speaking of a distinctive language, Yakuu, in favour of a new way of life, a new, unrelated language, Maa, as well as other cultural adaptations. A group of people who now identify themselves as Maasai – and would be so identified by outsiders – are only two generations away from being people who identified themselves very differently.

A similar process was underway in Rwanda and Burundi under Belgian rule. The colonial state demanded that Africans state their tribal affiliations on the documents required for the registration of births, for the pursuit of work, and for cross-border travel. The terms 'Tutsi' and 'Hutu', which, as we have seen, were derived from something more like class terminology than ethnicity, became tribes. Recording membership of one or other suddenly froze personal identity. And the Tutsi, largely because they were felt to be a racially superior people, became more favoured by the Belgians, enjoying greater access to mission education and to paid employment in the colonial bureaucracy. Colonial rule did not invent inequality and conflict. But it pushed it in dangerous, and ultimately disastrous, new directions.

During the era of European imperialism, the idea of 'tribe' encapsulated the otherness of Africans. But like many changes wrought by colonial conquest, the concept took root. Tribal affiliation (or to use a more polite but barely less loaded phrase, 'ethnicity') has in many places been embraced by Africans themselves, competing with kinship, with religion, and with nation as a framework of belonging. For some, it contained moral ideas rooted in remembered histories of the forging of communities and of states. For others, especially for politicians seeking to mobilize the support of regional constituencies, it became a tool used for the accumulation of power. As we will see later, struggles for slices of new national cakes have frequently been animated by a populism which derives much of its force from carefully nurtured sensitivities about supposed tribal or ethnic difference. In contemporary Africa, in short, the tension between the ideas of unity and diversity remains very much to the fore.

Chapter 3
Africa's past: historical sources

In common with historians of all places, historians of Africa have faced significant constraints. Before thinking about the particular problems faced by those attempting to recover Africa's past, it is important to stress that many such problems are shared with historians working on other parts of the world. The lives of ordinary working people, of women, or of children, for example, can be difficult and often impossible to capture and to interpret. But Africa presents its own challenges; some are formidable and not all have proved capable of resolution. In the process of addressing these challenges, historians have developed a range of methods which have not only increased the sophistication of African historical studies but have also added to the research techniques and the analytical armoury of the whole field of historical enquiry. While contributing to the store of knowledge about the past of humankind, historians of Africa have also been pioneers in the development of a battery of techniques which make modern historians more effective, sympathetic analysts of the lives of all our ancestors.

Evidence

The problem of evidence lay at the heart of the struggle to establish the field of African history in the 1950s and 1960s. Evidence necessarily underpins all historical research. Reliable sources provide knowledge of the past which then allows historians to analyse, to interpret, to compare, and to theorize. The absence of sources denies us that knowledge; and however attractive it can be, the substitution of what *should* have happened is supposition rather than scholarship. The postwar pioneers of African historical studies spent their early days fighting two big battles. One was waged against an academic establishment sceptical about the possibility of recovering Africa's past. Some recent observers have seen this conservatism as innately racist, a continuation of the attitudes faced by Du Bois and Hansberry in their efforts to claim a place for Africa in universal history. While some of the doubters might have been animated by racism, their objections were more frequently grounded in their understanding of what history was and thus what history could be. The other was a methodological assault against the established ways of 'doing' history, aimed at circumventing the dearth of written records for much of the continent. The two were closely related to one another. But while the former has, by and large, been won, the latter is far from over, demanding an ongoing inventiveness in the methods by which African history is researched and written.

Africa posed a real challenge at a particular conjuncture in the development of the discipline of history. By the mid-20th century, history had serious pretensions to being a discipline with its own (and for some, even a scientific) methodology, which sought to distance itself from antiquarianism, from anecdote, and from the mustering of mountains of supposed facts. At the core of that methodology lay the discovery of, and then the critical reading of, written documents: so-called 'primary sources'. These were to be found in the greatest abundance in archives and libraries. Reading that material in the writers' original languages, and if possible in its original manuscript form, reading it in the light of other sources, reading it 'between the lines' and 'against the grain', was what good historians did.

If written sources were the recognized raw materials of historical research, where did that leave historians with ambitions to write Africa's history? Most African languages were not transcribed languages; that is, they were spoken rather than written and read before the late 19th or the 20th century. But it was the earlier history of Africa that the pioneering historians wished above all to recover. Animated by the liberation of the continent from colonial rule, they sought to demonstrate to sceptical colleagues and to the wider world that the continent had a history of its own *before* European conquest – one that would serve as a template for the future. For many, sources generated by and about colonial conquest were irredeemably compromised. The authentic African voice, it was argued, was deafened or distorted in such material.

Much of what passed for African history before the 1950s fell within the established tradition of 'imperial history', a genre dominated by accounts of the African careers of European explorers, missionaries, proconsuls, and businessmen. Africans themselves tended to be regarded as objects rather than actors in the making and unmaking of European empires. Not all of that literature was inherently unsympathetic. In Britain and France especially, there was a lively variety of *anti*-imperialist imperial history which set out the malign impact of colonial conquest upon Africans. But this tradition was actually closer to imperial hagiography than it pretended to be. It too tended to objectify Africans and failed to take their long-term history and their own agency seriously. After all, there is not much to choose between being habitually disregarded or being regarded as a perennial victim. An analogy might be a situation in which we had no history of French or British people other than that incorporated into both favourable and hostile accounts of Roman expansion and early Christian conversion written by Romans. It was this sort of simplification and distortion that Africa's new historians set out to rectify.

Written sources: part 1

Indigenous written records were not entirely absent. One of the world's oldest scripts was that of ancient Egypt, the deciphering of which in the 1820s pushed the boundary between 'history' and 'prehistory' back thousands of years. 'It is ironic that we know more about cultural changes in the New Kingdom of the Pharao[h]s than we do about eighteenth-century Kuba cultural change, three thousand years and more later', Jan Vansina, the leading historian of the Kuba (a Central African kingdom), has lamented. Written language has also provided unusually rich sources for the history of Ethiopia. From the 5th century AD, the Ethiopian Coptic Church, one of the earliest Christian churches, used a written language called *Ge'ez* (whose script originated in ancient south Arabia) to translate the Bible and to record its landholdings, its prayers and healing formulae, and the lives of its saints. To these ecclesiastical documents were added royal chronicles and medieval compilations of law and history such as the *Kebre Negast*, 'The Glory of the Kings', the ideological charter of Ethiopian kingship.

The advance of Islam ensured that command of Arabic, the language of the Qur'an, was disseminated amongst the learned within its spreading domains. By the 8th century, precious fragments of information on sub-Saharan Africa begin to emerge from the accounts of Muslim travellers and geographers – sources that have proved crucial for recovering the early history of the sudanic kingdoms and of the Swahili city-states of the east coast. Yet these remain the fleeting impressions of outsiders (see Chapter 1). It is not until many centuries later that locally written Arabic chronicles appear south of the Sahara: first the 'Kilwa chronicle', recounting the history of the coastal town of Kilwa in present-day Tanzania (c. 1520), followed by Ahmad b. Furtuwa's account of the central sudanic state of Bornu (c. 1576), and then the two great 'Timbuktu chronicles', the *Ta'rikh al-fattash* (competed c. 1655) and al-Sa'di's *Ta'rikh al-sudan* (also c. 1655). From the 18th century,

10. Priests of the Ethiopian Orthodox Church, photographed in Eritrea displaying religious manuscripts, 1890s. From Ferdinando Martini, *Nell'Africa Italiana* (Milan, 1895)

moreover, Arabic script also became the basis for the transliteration of three major African languages, Hausa, Fulfulde, and Swahili.

Following the planting in 1652 of a Dutch colony at the Cape of Good Hope, in what became South Africa, we also have access to documents written in the Dutch language and increasingly in its developing local offspring, Afrikaans, a tongue nuanced by African languages, Portuguese, and Malay. The time-depth and copiousness of these sources has allowed historians of southern Africa to reconstruct some aspects of the past with a degree of detail which is hard to emulate in other parts of the continent south of the Sahara. In common with the accounts of Muslim visitors to black Africa – and also the great body of documentation generated by European traders, missionaries, soldiers, and explorers dating back to the 15th century – much of this material is one-sided, prejudiced, and misguided. It requires critical reading and careful analysis – like all historical sources, only more so.

The volume of documentation about Africans and, importantly, written by Africans themselves, expands dramatically once we reach the era of European imperialism in the 19th and 20th centuries. Much of this material, especially the latter, was generated by Christian missions. Even before the conquest and partition of Africa at the end of the 19th century, missionaries were spreading through many regions of the continent. Early on, converts were few, but Protestant missions in particular placed great importance on the translation of the Bible, of hymns, and of prayers into vernacular languages. In contrast with the Qur'an, which must ideally be heard and read in its original Arabic, Christianity's holy book welcomed translation. It was therefore often missionaries – both African and European – who took the lead in the transformation of many languages from oral to written forms of communication. The ultimate goal of this linguistic work was to convert Africans to Christianity. But it also resulted in bold new forms of written history, much of which was inspired by the narrative drive of the Bible itself. Christianity looked to a progressive future, but it also gave rise to new ways of thinking about the past.

This process emerged first in the Christianized, English-speaking, and self-consciously modernizing trading diaspora of 19th-century coastal West Africa. It took shape in two pioneering landmarks of African historiography: Samuel Johnson's *History of the Yorubas* (1921, but completed 1897) and Carl Christian Reindorf's *History of the Gold Coast and Asante* (1895). Both authors were ordained pastors working for Protestant missions: Johnson, the Anglican Church Missionary Society, and Reindorf, the Basel Mission Society of Switzerland. Johnson was ethnically Yoruba, the child of parents liberated from slave ships and landed in Sierra Leone, where he was born and educated. Reindorf was a Ga from the Accra region of the Gold Coast, whose paternal grandfather was a resident Danish trader. Both shared an enthusiasm for robust, evangelizing Christianity, for material and moral progress, and for British overrule, all of which they regarded as essential for the elimination of 'heathenism' and violent political divisions, and for the eventual emergence of African states as modern nations.

These extraordinary books combined dense ethnographic observation, traditions of origin, and detailed historical narratives constructed from a combination of personal experience, oral research, and, in Reindorf's case, the reading of old European written accounts. Johnson's work had a profound impact on notions of Yoruba identity, serving as the template for a unified 'national' history while at the same time spurring into print other local historians uncomfortable with his bias towards the city-states of Oyo and Ibadan. Importantly, he and Reindorf wrote in English, in part because mastery of that language was seen to be a tool of progress and in part because their envisaged audience included Europeans. But both books were largely ignored beyond their respective regions of origin, unable to make a dent in the prevailing European wisdom that tropical Africa possessed no recoverable history. It is only in recent decades that scholars have begun fully to

11. Translating the Bible. A team of Basel missionaries and African pastors, including, second from right, Rev. Carl Christian Reindorf, work on revisions to the Ga translation of the Bible at Abokobi, Gold Coast (present-day Ghana), circa 1900–2. Photograph by Max Shultz

appreciate just how important they are, both as primary sources and as pioneering works of historical scholarship in their own right.

The transliteration (and with it the standardization) of African languages continued into the period of colonial rule. So too did the writing down of local historical traditions (see Chapter 5). European administrators in many areas emphasized the use of the vernacular to facilitate the collection of intelligence about, and the transmission of instructions to, their African subjects. The languages of command in British colonial armies in West and East Africa, for example, were Hausa and Swahili, respectively. And many early ethnographers, some of whose work was intimately involved in the business of assisting the colonial project, were avid recorders of African languages. All of this was as much the work of the first generations of Africans schooled in the Western fashion; a great deal of the linguistic, ethnographic, and historical information published under the names of Europeans was the product of the hard work of frequently anonymous 'African informants'.

The drunken king: oral tradition

The pioneering generation of Africanist historians did not dispute the central significance of written sources. But given the enormous size of the continent and the great depth of its history, such sources were few and far between. And what kind of African history would emerge if it was to be based upon a documentary record laid down for the most part by visitors from Europe and the Islamic Mediterranean rather than by Africans themselves? Reliance upon such evidence, it was felt, risked repeating the ignorance, objectification, condescension, and essentialism all too apparent in the treatment of 'natives' in imperial history. Rather, they began to dispute the conflation of 'source' with 'document', to suggest that the idea of evidence need not be solely synonymous with written texts.

Research experience, listening to Africans speaking about the past, led them to the notion that oral traditions might be taken seriously. Not to be confused with 'oral history', that is, the recording of an individual's own memories, oral tradition was defined as the passing down from generation to generation of events that extended into the deep past. This was undoubtedly radical. Historians were no strangers to written versions of what appeared to have been older oral accounts: Homer's *Iliad* and *Odyssey*, the Norse *Sagas*, and *Beowulf* were, for example, mainstays of Western culture. But modern historians had tried to distinguish themselves from their romantic intellectual predecessors (who had been much occupied with substantiating such canonical texts by excavating the supposed sites of Troy or the Cretan labyrinth) by regarding these ancient narratives as myths and, in the new psychologically inflected language, as 'archetypal'.

Nevertheless, anxiety about flawed documentary sources drew more and more scholars away from metropolitan libraries and archives and into Africa's towns and villages in search of living repositories of authentic historical narrative. Kings, chiefs, elders, Muslim scholars, specialist guardians of court histories, and professional bards such as the Mande *jeliw* were quizzed about the past, and considerably detailed accounts emerged. Some of these discoveries were of the already discovered: oral traditions had been recorded by Johnson, Reindorf, and other pioneering African scholars. Yet the argument was made that these traditions could be read in the same sorts of ways as historians read written documents, a claim elaborated by Jan Vansina in *Oral Tradition* (1965, but first published in French 1961). This was a big claim and a brave one, subversive of conventional historical practice. It had a significant impact upon not only the recovery of African history but also that of other traditionally non-literate societies in the Pacific, the Americas, and elsewhere. The new African history was also read with interest by social historians frustrated by the difficulty of recapturing 'history from below' in ostensibly literate societies; its methodological influence is evident in the pages of the radical *History Workshop Journal* from the late 1960s.

Yet oral traditions, as Vansina recognized from the outset, were far from straightforward. They were generated within particular cultures and strongly shaped by local aesthetic preferences, with narratives often advancing by way of spiritual or magical transformation rather than incremental chronological change. Early attempts to date events – typically by applying average lengths of reigns to the 'king lists' common to many traditions – proved abortive and were quickly abandoned. 'That African dynasties might have exhibited greater order . . . than unpredictable struggles over power elsewhere in the world proved a vain hope', Joseph Miller notes in a recent appraisal. It became apparent too that those very struggles for power shaped and continued to reshape versions of the past. Oral narratives were certainly unwritten texts, but they were only rarely reliable vehicles of factual information. They were instead increasingly regarded as fascinating sources for intellectual historians keen to understand the cultural contexts of meaning rather than the sequence and causes of events. An analogy might be our modern opinion of Walter Raleigh's *History of the World* (1614) as an unreliable guide to world history before 150 BC (this was as far as Raleigh got before his execution) but as a text that provides insight into the understandings of history by educated people in England in the early 17th century.

These issues can be illustrated by considering one of Africa's most intensively scrutinized oral traditions of origin, that of the Luba kingdom in the present-day Democratic Republic of Congo. Like the story of Sunjata as performed by Mande *jeliw*, the Luba tradition is a popular epic recited as a sequence of free-form narrative episodes by specialists called *inabanza*s, 'men of memory'. The order of the episodes is marked on mnemonic devices called *lukasa*s, 'memory boards' studded with beads and cowrie shells that are held by members of the *bambudye* secret society. The central storyline, based on a version told by one famous *inabanza*, Kabata (c. 1860 to c. 1950), goes something like this:

> As the lands of the Luba were first being inhabited, there emerged a cruel, red-skinned king who took the name Nkongolo (lit. 'the rainbow'). Nkongolo was incestuous, sterile, loudmouthed, and drunken. A handsome, dark-skinned, and cultured hunter from the east, Mbidi Kiluwe crossed the Lomani river into Nkongolo's domains, where he married the king's two sisters. One of them, Bulanda, fathered a son, Kalala Ilunga ('Ilunga the warrior'), who grew up in his uncle's village. Conflict developed between the two, and Nkongolo decided to kill Kalala Ilunga. But the latter fled back across the river to the east, where he raised an army. Returning, he overthrew and executed his despotic uncle, instituted sacred kingship, and founded the royal dynasty of the Luba heartland, *Luba Shankadi*.

Scholarly interpretations of this and similar traditions in the kingdoms of the savanna woodlands of Central Africa have shifted over time. Early historical readings tended to take them, if not quite literally, then as preserving kernels of real events, some even attempting to provide approximate dates for the tales of migration, political violence, and state-building. But anthropologists argued that such stories were not history but myth, cosmological speculation about timeless, 'structural' opposites. Thus, Nkongolo can be seen to personify the life-threatening chaos of the pre-dynastic order only partially removed from nature, whereas Mbidi Kiluwe and Kalala Ilunga represent fertility and 'culture'. By the 1990s, historians had refined their analysis, countering that traditions of origin were really about the ongoing legitimization of political power at the time they were told. They were ideological statements made by the winners of political struggles, not the losers.

Is there a middle ground? Possibly, suggests John Yoder, the author of a book on the Kanyok, a people who fell under the cultural and political influence of the expanding Luba kingdom. The Luba tradition of origin, he suggests, is neither a chronicle of actual events nor simply a reflection of contemporary power, but a commentary on the meanings of historical change. It may not be 'history' as conventionally understood in the West, but it is *about* history as perceived by those people who call themselves Luba. Two things are sure: in the Luba-speaking region of southern Congo, the popular epic of Nkongolo and Kalala Ilunga will continue to be told. And amongst scholars, the debate will go on.

Embracing 'the other': history and other disciplines

Acknowledging the paucity of written sources might have been painful, but it was of huge importance to the ways in which the study of African history developed. It stimulated Africa's historians from the outset to become adept at engaging with other disciplines. From its foundation in 1960, the field's pioneer journal, the *Journal of African History*, carried articles on linguistics, on physical anthropology, and, most prominently, on archaeology. This openness was radical, but it was also a reflection of the fact that very little was known about the history of the continent. Accordingly, a good deal of research at this stage was taken up with trying to answer some pretty basic questions of periodization and historical geography. This was a demanding task given the great time-depth and diversity of Africa's human history and the principled ambition to chronicle the broad sweep of its past. For these reasons, the transition from hunting and gathering to settled agriculture (the 'food-producing revolution') and the dissemination of iron-working, processes which historians of Europe would have considered to fall into the realm of 'prehistory', were regarded as central concerns of the new African history.

Perhaps the most important and sustained interdisciplinary relationship, however, was that with social anthropology. Like many intimate relationships, this grew out of an earlier mutual suspicion that sometimes bordered on hostility. Historians were content to mine colonial-era ethnographies for data. But many harboured suspicions about the implied timelessness and self-contained quality of tribal groups moored in the 'ethnographic present'. In turn, some anthropologists were sceptical about the ambitions of historians. Others were perplexed by the latter's tendency to emphasize state-building at the expense of kinship and culture. But as the two disciplines evolved, they came to cross-fertilize one another. Just as the new African history first blossomed in the climate of anti-colonial nationalism, so too did anthropology change with the times, entering a period of self-reflection and critiquing its own origins as a 'colonial science'. In recent years, as more and more anthropologists have sought a temporal dimension for their work (many now combining 'fieldwork' with archival research), historians have embraced a range of issues (religion and belief, for example) that hitherto had been left to the former.

Not all of these excursions into other disciplines proved to be quite so rewarding. A great deal of effort was expended on the mastery of historical linguistics. Some linguists claimed that a variety of techniques could be used to date the dissemination of Africa's languages. If languages were attached to cultures, might one be able to use historical linguistics to demonstrate the physical movement of peoples? Efforts here focused on an attempt to understand the extraordinary distribution of the so-called Bantu languages, some 600 related languages spread over almost the entire southern half of the continent. Mobilizing linguistics, archaeological research (especially on pottery styles and iron-making technology), and oral traditions (the stories of migration embedded in epics like that of the Luba), historians developed a model that became known as the 'Bantu expansion': one, continuous mass migration of iron-using agriculturalists who 'broke through' the equatorial forest from the northwest, overwhelming original populations of hunter-gatherers.

This kind of reasoning chimed in neatly with the attractions of physical migration as an explanation of cultural change. There was nothing particularly African about this: historians had earlier been busy dragging Celts from central Europe into France and the British Isles and 'Aryans' into India. Our understandings of cultural diffusion are now more subtle. While there is abundant evidence for the spread of languages, cultures, and technologies in Africa, as elsewhere, the 'Bantu expansion' model has been revealed as too simplistic. Rather than a sudden, massive movement of population, it is more likely to have ebbed and flowed over two millennia, with the transfer of ideas just as important as the migration of people. This false start in our understanding of early Africa was of no lasting significance. But it consumed a good deal of energy, not least because the linguistic data and techniques were complex and mastery of them was time-consuming.

Archaeology proved to be a more rewarding, if occasionally troublesome, bed-fellow. On other continents, archaeology had provided a good deal of evidence about human societies before the emergence of written records. Much of what was known about the history of the ancient Mediterranean, the Near East, Neolithic Europe, and of pre-Columbian America had been documented by archaeologists. The archaeology of the later 20th century remained romantic, as the pages of *National Geographic* demonstrate; but it was now a science-based discipline, and this was attractive to historians of Africa whose thin documentary record provided them with few chronological clues. The older tradition of stratigraphy (the recording of the 'layers of time' revealed by the excavation of a settlement site), plus newer techniques of radiocarbon dating and tree-ring dating, provided exciting opportunities for the dating of human remains, settlements, and the artefacts of material culture – and from the resulting data the construction of narratives of long-term change.

Much has been achieved in sketching out the contours of Africa's deep past. Yet the answers that archaeologists have been able to come up with have still often disappointed historians. Huge swathes of the continent, notably the equatorial forest zone, have barely been surveyed, let alone subjected to extensive excavation.

Quite simply, sites of potential importance are hard to find. The historical sparseness of population in many regions ensured that large concentrations of people – that is, cities – were relatively rare. Rarer still were towns built of the kinds of materials that endure over time. Even the 'ancient' mud mosques of the sahelian cities of Jenne, Timbuktu, and Gao have been repeatedly reconstructed over the centuries. With very few exceptions (notably the famous remains of 'Great Zimbabwe' and the 'stone towns' on the Swahili coast), African settlements were built of readily available wood or mud. Using these materials was labour-saving, but they were biodegradable in the extreme; the eroding ferocity of desert sand-storms, heavy rainfall, and the subversive activities of termites are the natural enemies of built environments. Tropical Africa is notable for its absence of 'ruins', and the consequent lack of glamour is not conducive to the kinds of economic support generated by the thought of lost cities and hidden treasures.

As we have seen with regard to Jenne-jeno, archaeologists do not necessarily need large amounts of material remains above ground in order to make startling discoveries about the patterns of the past. But even modern dating techniques remain blunt instruments, and data must be contextualized carefully in order to avoid speculative claims with potentially revolutionary implications for established chronologies. Claims that discoveries in the Termit region of Niger show early, indigenous innovation in iron smelting, for example, remain fiercely contested decades after radiocarbon dates were calculated. In short, archaeology in Africa faces huge technical and logistical constraints. Some of this has been the result of political instability, some of the cost of fieldwork. Both have had an especially damaging impact upon the few active departments of archaeology in African universities. The priority, according to Susan Keech McIntosh, must be 'the urgent recovery of *some* subset of information about the African archaeological past before it all disappears in the face of development, agriculture, or looting'.

Despite its limitations, archaeology has been crucial to the study of Africa's art history. As a discipline, art history is distinct from history – although the two are closely related. Whereas historians deal mainly with texts, whether written or oral, art historians examine forms and images. Yet forms and images have great historical relevance. As 'creations of minds and hands rooted in specific historical and social contexts', writes Henry John Drewal, they are 'signs of the times and shapes of thought'. But how does form become 'art'? As with other hold-all terms for aspects of human culture (like 'religion'), scholars have needed to be careful not to impose Western concepts on African realities. Some African languages have no specific word for 'art'. Others do, such as Yoruba, in which the term *ona* encompasses a broad range of evocative material transformations designed to move and to enlighten the viewer. Recently, scholars have begun to challenge the exclusive (and sometimes Eurocentric) connotations of the term 'art' by redefining their field as 'visual culture', thereby broadening its scope to include popular forms such as film and television, photography, clothing, and body decoration.

Although sculpture from West Africa began to arrive in Europe as early as the 1470s, it was only with colonial conquest that an awareness of 'African art' developed in the West. One key moment was the looting by a British military force of a hoard of artefacts from Benin (in present-day Nigeria) in 1897. Many of these, especially the famous 'Benin bronzes' (mostly actually made of brass), found their way into museums and collections across Europe. Their striking appearance sparked expeditions aimed specifically at collecting art objects, such as that undertaken on behalf of the British Museum by the ethnographer Emil Torday to the Kuba kingdom of southern Congo in 1907–9. Another was the discovery of sculpture from West and Central Africa by Pablo Picasso and other Paris-based avant-garde artists in about 1905. Just as African music transformed 20th-century popular music, so too did the export of African plastic art contribute to the modern revolution in concepts of form. As excited by the apparent disregard for naturalism as they would be by the wild sonorities of Duke Ellington, modernist artists and thinkers drew freely – and loosely – on what they perceived as the robust and liberating 'primitivism' of African culture.

For European devotees of 'primitive art', however, it was form alone that mattered, not function or context – let alone history. Throughout the colonial period and beyond, African artefacts flowed into Western museums and private collections, but few were dated and fewer still were attributed to individual artists or even to particular workshops. Instead, they were ordered according to typical tribal styles: 'Luba stool', 'Dogon mask', 'Kuba statue', 'Kota ancestral figure', and so forth. Such ethnic attributions were often as simplistic and misleading as the very notion of timeless, hermetically sealed 'tribes' itself. This has frustrated the emergence of an art history of Africa, both in its own right and in ways that might assist historians in the task of reconstructing the changing textures of culture over space and over time.

History's engagement with art history in Africa remains in its infancy, but the potential is enormous. Many art historians are now taking the 'history' part of their job description as seriously as the 'art', while more historians look to art as a reflection of – and even as an integral component of – broader patterns of change. Art objects are not 'texts'. But neither, with careful contextualization, need they be mute. Gradually, scholars are replacing Western aesthetic appreciation with indigenous African perceptions, timeless tribal iconography with more fluid regional 'streams of tradition', and a narrow focus on 'fine art' with a broader, more inclusive embrace of visual cultures. There is growing understanding, too, of the intimate relationship between plastic art and performing art, most obviously that in West and Central Africa between mask and masquerade. These developments are becoming apparent not only in scholarly writing but in major exhibitions of African art, such as the *Africa: The Art of a Continent* retrospective staged in London in 1995, and *Africa Remix: Contemporary Art of a Continent* in 2005.

12. Art and historical memory. An official at the court of the Kuba king Kot aPe (1902–16) holds a dynastic sculpture (*ndop*) portraying the 18th-century king MishaaPelyeeng aNce, now in the British Museum. Photograph taken by Emil Torday or M. W. Hilton-Simpson at the Kuba capital Nsheng (in present-day Democratic Republic of Congo) in 1909

Written sources: part 2

All of this methodological innovation and transdisciplinary eclecticism has enriched the field of African history. At the end of the day, however, written sources remain as crucial for the recovery of the continent's past as they do for that of any other part of the world. The availability and nature of the evidence dictates the kinds of history that can – and cannot – be written. So it is important to make the point that the volume and the range of written sources have, generally speaking, increased significantly since the days when the postwar pioneers of modern African history first ventured into the archives. And as the amount of source material has expanded, so too have attitudes towards it shifted.

The re-evaluation of records generated by outsiders has underlined not only their flaws but also their value. With regards to the travel literature, both in European languages and in Arabic, modern critical editions have exposed some of these texts as armchair volumes, assemblages of the writings of others. But it has also shown that many are unique, eye-witness accounts by people who had spent long periods in Africa and had real insights into local cultures, politics, and sometimes even the events of the past. Likewise, the accounts of missionaries, once regarded by many as cultural imperialists and the enablers of colonial conquest, are now seen as providing vital insights into the complex processes of religious conversion and cultural change. Then there is the documentary residue of the slave trade. It is a painful irony that one of the largest and potentially most valuable collections of writing about Africans is to be found in the recently compiled database of slave voyages across the Atlantic (see Chapter 4).

Between the state archives of the ex-imperial powers and those of African nations, virtually the entire official record of the era of colonial rule is now open for consultation. These sources have also been revealed as being less biased and marred by racial arrogance than once thought: more a multitude of discordant voices than the monotonous drone of imperial hegemony. Many of these are African voices, of those who accommodated themselves to colonial rule as well as those who struggled against it, including some of women, of the poor, and even of slaves. The much sought-after 'African voice' often comes through vividly in the huge bodies of court records – long recognized as a vital resource for social historians everywhere. These include the proceedings of so-called 'native courts' operated by indigenous African jurists, such as the sequence (in Arabic) of the Zanzibar courts running from 1880 to 1960.

The critical use of imaginative literature can also alleviate the relative lack of African biography and autobiography, helping to flesh out the otherwise two-dimensional depiction of men and women in many sources. The Nigerian Nobel laureate Wole Soyinka's trilogy *Ake* (1981), *Isara* (1990), and *Ibadan* (1994), for example, provides us with an unsurpassed history of a family living through turbulent colonial and postcolonial times based upon family papers, his and others' personal recollections, as well as poetic imagination and an animating sense of the dramatic. And there is no better account of the austere lives in mid-20th-century London of the young African nationalists who were eventually to lead their countries to independence than South African novelist Peter Abrahams' *Wreath for Udomo* (1956). Like plastic art, literature is both a reflection of and a component of historical change.

On the negative side, many African archives are in a bad state. While history was deemed to be an important aspect of nation-building in the 1960s, it is now too often regarded as an unnecessary luxury by politicians and civil servants with other priorities – be they laudable or self-serving. The conservation of old documents, letters, newspapers, maps, photographs, newsreels, and suchlike, is costly and often neglected, leaving many collections at the mercy of the tropical climate and insect population. The accession and cataloguing of new state papers has also stalled in some countries, with the result that their archives have remained essentially as the record of colonial rule alone. These assets might have been more strenuously defended had they been used by generations of local historians. But many African universities have also suffered financial neglect in the era of economic decline and political turmoil from the 1970s. In the worst cases of state collapse and infrastructural breakdown, great chunks of the record of the past remain in danger of crumbling away.

But it would be overly pessimistic to end on this note. Certainly, before the wider expansion of literacy in the 20th century, we are often prevented from accessing the experiences of individual women and men and how those experiences were understood. The lack of evidence continues to tempt historians towards essentialism, towards generalizations about the thoughts and feelings of large numbers of people. Yet many collections of documents remain underutilized, while others continue to be discovered. North African and Turkish archives, for example, contain large amounts of neglected material on sub-Saharan Africa, while the Ahmad Baba Historical Documentation and Research Centre in Timbuktu (established in 1973) now contains some 20,000 locally authored Arabic texts, reaffirming the role of that ancient city on the edge of the Sahara as a centre of scholarship and learning. Historical research in Africa is a real challenge, but new generations of students both from the continent and beyond continue to uncover such new sources and to re-read old ones in pursuit of the past.

Chapter 4
Africa in the world

Our focus in this chapter shifts from the sources and methods used by historians to some of the histories they have come up with. It also shifts from the particularities of Africa's past to its engagement with the broader sweep of world history. How does the history of Africa fit into that of the rest of the world? Has the course of the African past been determined mainly by forces internal to the continent itself, or by those emanating from beyond its shores? To what extent have African peoples been able to shape their own destinies?

These questions remain as knotty today as when the academic study of African history began 50 years ago. Indeed, in this era of accelerating globalization, they may be more pressing than ever. For Africa's pioneer historians, the task was to explode the European myth of the continent as a timeless, insular realm, isolated from the main currents of human progress. There can be no denying the advances made on this score. At the start of the 21st century, however, Africa is once again seen by many in the West (and in 'the East') as marginal to world affairs – and becoming increasingly so. As other parts of the old Third World, especially the rising economic powers of China and India, emerge onto the global stage, Africa seems to be being left behind. Mired in poverty, debt, corruption, and conflict, the continent is still perceived as 'particular', as beyond the pale.

Getting the balance right between the infinitely varied textures of local history on the one hand and broader, impersonal forces of change on the other has been an issue for historians of all regions of the world. But the need to overcome the hoary racial myths of the past while at the same time capturing the distinctiveness of the African historical experience has made it a particular concern for Africanists. By emphasizing the autonomy of African history, the danger is to underline the old idea of the continent's essential difference and isolation. But by emphasizing Africa's interconnectedness with the world beyond, the danger is to submerge what has been distinctive about its history in a unilinear process dominated by 'the rise of the West'. This problem has been compounded by a growing anxiety about the 'appropriation' of indigenous forms of knowledge and representation by the Western discipline of history. How suited is academic history, with its rules of evidence and its aspirations to 'universal truths', to represent the African past on its own terms and according to its own logic?

Even where the West does not dominate the historical narrative, Africa's role in world history remains tenuous at best. C. A. Bayly's book *The Birth of the Modern World* (2004) is a case in point. Bayly, a historian of South Asia, sets out to challenge the established Eurocentric narrative of the emergence of 'modernity' by relocating the process from the West to a broader, interconnected world (once again, we can see how contemporary issues – 'globalization' – spur historians to reconsider the past). But sub-Saharan Africa is conspicuous in his account only by its absence: consigned still, in an otherwise groundbreaking work, to the margins of history.

The local and the global are not mutually exclusive. Much recent writing on Africa has focused on exploring the interaction between the two, on the ambiguous, 'liminal' zones where they have collided and on the distinctive new cultural forms that have been thrown up as a result. These forms, it can be argued, are as modern as the modernity once associated exclusively with Western progress. Neither is modernity necessarily to be seen as a good thing. A leading French Africanist scholar, Jean-François Bayart, has argued that the historic difficulties facing would-be state-builders in consolidating power over populations within Africa has led to their pursuing what he calls strategies of 'extraversion', that is, 'mobilizing resources from their (possibly unequal) relationship with the external environment'. The most striking example of this strategy is the prominent role played by some African rulers in the overseas slave trade, although Bayart, as a political scientist, is concerned more with the venality of much of the continent's contemporary political leadership.

The internal *versus* the external, local *versus* global, the particular *versus* the universal: by themselves these are simply frameworks around which to organize and to think about historical evidence. Only occasionally does the accumulation of evidence force a fundamental shift in thinking one way or the other. We saw one such shift confirmed by the archaeological findings at Jenne-jeno, which played a big part in pointing historians to internal rather than external factors in explaining the rise of urbanism and 'complex societies' in the sudanic zone of West Africa. In this chapter, we further consider the interconnections between Africa and the world by looking at four major themes in the continent's history: the impact of Islam and Christianity, the slave trade, the African diaspora, and the tumultuous changes of the 19th century.

A Kongolese Saint Anthony: world religions and Africa

On 2 July 1706, at Evululu in the kingdom of Kongo (in the north of modern Angola), Dona Beatriz Kimpa Vita was burned at the stake. The 22-year-old Beatriz's crimes were heresy and witchcraft. Two years earlier, she had declared herself to be possessed by St Anthony and had begun a popular religious movement aimed at reunifying the kingdom following its descent into civil war in the 1660s. In a campaign recorded by Italian Capuchin missionaries, Beatriz preached a radical reinterpretation of Christian history, declaring

72

that Jesus, Mary, and St Francis – the Capuchins' patron – were all in fact Kongolese. Turning to a catechism translated into the Kikongo language in 1624, she took as her central text the prayer to the Virgin Mary, the Salve Regina, changing the wording so it became the 'Salve Antoniana'. At its height, her movement took control of the old Kongo capital, São Salvador, but shortly thereafter Beatriz fell into the hands of one of the warring royal factions. Following her execution, the cycle of political violence continued, with many Antonians suffering the fate of countless Kongolese peasants before them: sold by warlords into the Atlantic slave trade.

The slave trade we shall return to shortly. First, let us consider the tragedy of Beatriz Kimpa Vita as an episode in the history of Christianity. For those who associate the coming of Christianity to Africa with Victorian missionaries like David Livingstone, the existence of Catholic Africans in the 17th century may seem surprising. Yet Catholicism in Kongo dates back to 1491, when Portuguese mariners delivered the first priests to the kingdom and Nzinga a Nkuwu was baptized as King João I, its first Christian ruler. Under João's son, Afonso I (1509–43), Catholicism became the official state cult, mobilized by the king against rivals who wielded *kindoki*, indigenous ritual power. It also began to spread from the aristocracy to ordinary people, where it fused with elements of *kindoki* to create a local 'folk Catholicism' apparent at the time of Beatriz and beyond. Thus, Beatriz's possession by St Anthony must be seen in the light of her role as a *nganga*, a 'spirit medium', while baptism was desired by many as protection against *ndoki*, 'witches' (which she herself was accused of being).

Kongo was a rare success in the history of European attempts to plant Christianity in Atlantic Africa during the era of the slave trade. Yet the way in which Catholicism was reinterpreted and reimagined by Kongolese believers was quite typical of the integration of Christianity and of Islam into local African cultures – and, indeed, of the appropriation of indigenous spiritual resources. For both so-called world religions, this process of appropriation, or

13. Christianity in Kongo. A Capuchin missionary celebrates Mass in the Soyo province of the kingdom of Kongo (present-day Angola). Watercolour by Bernadino Ignazio, a missionary in Soyo in 1743–7, from the manuscript 'Missione in prattica. Padri cappuccino ne Regni di Congo, Angola et

'Africanization', was underway almost from their very beginnings. It continues to the present day, and constitutes one of the most dynamic developments in Africa's social and intellectual history.

The historical depth and complexity of Africa's engagement with world religions should not be underestimated. North Africa was an important early centre of Christianity, which spread first to Egypt and then on to the rest of Roman Africa. From the 4th century, the Egyptian Coptic Church (a breakaway from the Orthodox Church at Constantinople) also sent missionaries south to Aksum in Ethiopia and to Nubia. It was in Ethiopia where the faith became most firmly embedded in local society, taking on a highly distinctive form that included elements of ancient Judaism. Political legitimacy came to turn on descent from the biblical King Solomon, a claim enshrined in the *Kebre Negast*, 'The Glory of the Kings'. Christian warrior-kings, in alliance with equally tough-minded monastic holy men, pushed the frontiers of the faith throughout the highlands, defending their new Zion against pagan and Muslim enemies alike. While Christianity in North Africa and then in Nubia succumbed to the expansion of Islam, the Ethiopian Church survived into modern times.

Islam too took on localized forms during its passage to the Maghrib, across the Sahara, and down the East African coast. This does not mean that it became 'watered down' from its fundamentals by being absorbed into existing belief systems. As David Robinson, a leading historian of Muslim societies in Africa, points out, 'Africanization' (or, more correctly, Berber-ization, Swahili-ization, Mandinka-ization, etc.) does *not* mean the creation of an essentialized 'African Islam' – the inferior *Islam noir* of the French colonial imagination. Like Christianity, Islam in Africa was expressed in a huge diversity of forms, ranging from heterodox Sufi orders to the most orthodox reformist movements. A striking early example of the latter were the Almoravids, a militant Berber movement that in the 11th century swept out of the western Sahara to 'purify' the faith. Forging a new dynasty in Morocco and Spain ruled from

Marrakesh, they were the precursors of later West African *jihad* movements that sought to create Islamic states cleansed of lingering 'pagan' influences.

In contrast to North Africa, the growth of Islam in the *bilad as-Sudan* did not stem primarily from political conquest or the Arabization of local cultures. For many centuries, it remained a minority faith in overwhelmingly 'pagan' lands. Even in states where ruling elites converted to Islam, such as medieval Mali or Songhay, local believers often sought accommodation with established ways of life rather than seeking to overthrow them. Yet at the same time, they became part of something bigger: Muslim space, Muslim time, and Muslim scriptural culture, focused on the Qur'an. Like the claim of Ethiopian kings to Solomonic descent (and Beatriz's claim of a Kongolese Jesus), many sought to anchor themselves historically in the faith by inventing genealogies that went back to the Prophet or his companions. Such attachment brought *baraka* ('blessing'). It also conferred a broader identity, one that transcended local communities and, by the 20th century, complicated emerging ideas of what it meant to be 'African'.

These issues: conversion, the 'Africanization' of Islam and Christianity, the creation of new forms of ritual knowledge and of new identities, perceptions of the world embedded in ideas such as 'witchcraft', have emerged in recent years at the cutting-edge of much historical research. Previously, religion in Africa was a topic left mainly to anthropologists (in the case of indigenous belief) or to religious studies departments (in the case of the world religions). Yet the enormous expansion of Christianity and Islam on the continent throughout the 20th century, together with the diverse localized forms that both have taken, has meant that the theme of religious encounter is one that historians can no longer ignore. The vast majority of Africa's population now profess to be either Muslim or Christian, with the overall numbers of each about equal. From a 21st-century viewpoint, religious affiliation represents perhaps the most striking historical engagement between Africa and the world.

That said, many of the most important questions about religious change in Africa continue to be asked by anthropologists. Wyatt MacGaffey, for example, has been influential in extending the history of the encounter between Christianity and the Kongo into the 20th century, tracing the rise of modern movements such as that inspired by the 1920s evangelist Simon Kimbangu – the heir to the prophetic vision of Beatriz Kimpa Vita. The dynamics of religious belief and practice, involving questions of how people in the past thought about the world and their place in it, are tricky to reconstruct and often controversial. One important debate has arisen around the response of Africans to Christian missions. In *Of Revelation and Revolution*, a study of 19th-century European missions amongst the Tswana peoples of present-day Botswana and South Africa, anthropologists Jean Comaroff and John Comaroff argue that evangelization represented nothing less than a 'colonization of the consciousness'. Christianity, in short, was the key ingredient of a hegemonic European worldview imposed upon its converts.

Others have seen things differently. One is J. D. Y. Peel, an anthropologist whose work focuses on Yoruba Christianity. In *Religious Encounter and the Making of the Yoruba*, Peel sees Christian conversion not as a colonization of the consciousness but as a process of active appropriation. Yoruba Christians, he demonstrates, strove to make the faith their own, incorporating it into local narratives of progress and in doing so reshaping the meaning and the content of 'Yoruba' itself. This difference in interpretation may be explained to some extent by the contrasting historical experiences of the Tswana, on the one hand, and the Yoruba, on the other. It may also be due to the nature of the sources available. The Comaroffs relied heavily on the writings of European missionaries, while Peel made great use of the diaries of Yoruba evangelists. But it also reflects a more fundamental debate concerning the extent of African agency in the creation of the transnational networks that have shaped the history of the modern world.

Way of death: the slave trade in African history

Nowhere is this debate more pronounced or more impassioned than with regard to the Atlantic slave trade. It is not difficult to understand why. Between the 1440s, when Portuguese mariners first began to kidnap and to purchase Africans, and 1867, the year of the last recorded slaving voyage to the Americas, some 12 million men, women, and children were turned into commodities and exported from the continent. This bare statistic only goes so far in capturing the violence, the devastation, and the degradation initiated by what anti-slave trade campaigners called this 'odious commerce'. It does not include the countless lives lost through slave raiding, warfare, and social breakdown within Africa, nor those captives who succumbed to disease or maltreatment before embarkation. Neither does it include those enslaved but not exported, as Atlantic commerce acted as a catalyst for the expansion and intensification of slavery in African societies. And it does not include those Africans who were born and then died in the cauldron of the American slave system. Joseph Miller captures in one phrase this history of systemized suffering: the slave trade in Angola, he writes, became a 'way of death'.

The Atlantic trade, moreover, was not the only African slave trade. By the end of the first millennium AD, captives were also being taken across the Sahara, over the Red Sea, and from the coast of East Africa, destined for servitude in North Africa and the Mediterranean, in the Middle East, and throughout the Indian Ocean. Much of this commerce was in the hands of Muslims. Far less is known about it than the Atlantic trade, and the rarity of statistical data means that the overall numbers of enslaved can only be guessed at. Yet historians estimate that over more than 1,000 years, these combined trades may have involved a similar number of victims: perhaps another 12 million Africans. The 'Muslim' trades differed from the Atlantic trade in one important respect: whereas the victims of the latter were bound overwhelmingly for productive labour in the plantations and mines of the Americas, most victims of the former were destined for some form of domestic servitude, including concubinage. Twice as many African men as women were therefore transported across the Atlantic, whereas it is estimated that twice as many women as men were carried to the Muslim world.

When concerted research on the Atlantic slave trade began in the 1960s, the first priority was simply getting the numbers straight. One sometimes still reads wildly inflated figures like 20 million, or even 50 million, Africans having traversed the so-called Middle Passage. These do a disservice to decades of painstaking investigation – as well as to the memory of those who did fall victim to the slavers. The overall magnitude of the trade was confirmed in 1999 with the landmark publication of *The Trans-Atlantic Slave Trade: A Database on CD-ROM*, which details more than 27,000 slaving voyages from Africa to the New World from 1527 to 1867. Research on the Middle Passage itself continues – on the more than 55 shipboard rebellions, for example, that are recorded between 1699 and 1845, of which that on the *Amistad* is only the most famous. But historians of Africa are now shifting their attention to slaving frontiers within the continent. The ongoing Nigerian Hinterland Project, part of a UNESCO-sponsored 'Slave Routes' project, seeks to trace the origins of the millions of captives who were marched over the centuries from an enormous catchment area reaching deep into the savanna to ports of embarkation on the so-called 'Slave Coast' (modern Togo and Bénin) and Nigeria.

Assessing the role of the overseas slave trade in African history has proved hugely complex. For a start, its magnitude varied enormously over space and time. The Atlantic trade impacted on different regions of the West African coast – from Senegal down to Angola – to differing degrees over the four centuries of its operation. By the 19th century, it had also extended around the Cape of Good Hope to Mozambique, where it overlapped with the expanding Indian Ocean trade. What was the long-term demographic impact of the loss of population? To what extent was it responsible for

14. A 'coffle' of slaves (from the Arabic *kafila*, 'caravan') observed on 16 March 1850 chained together outside the Portuguese fort at Ouidah (in present-day Bénin), from F. E. Forbes, *Dahomey and the Dahomans* (London, 1851)

Africa's modern 'underdevelopment'? Then there is the question of the relationship between the overseas trade and the institution of slavery within Africa. Did the demand from overseas tap into existing systems of servitude? Or was slavery in Africa caused by – or at least transformed and intensified by – overseas demand? Finally, in what ways did the slave trade reshape regional political landscapes? What was the role of Africans themselves in the making of Atlantic commerce?

These are only some of the more important lines of inquiry. There is no space here even to summarize the range of possible answers, so let's step back and think about them in the context of our theme of Africa in world history. All of these issues to some extent turn on the problem of 'getting the balance right' between the internal and the external, between the agency of Africans and the impact of global ces. The slave trade was barbaric and exploitative, a crime against humanity. But by emphasizing these features, the tendency has been to portray Africa and Africans simply as passive victims. In an important work of revision, *Africa and Africans in the Making of the Atlantic World*, John Thornton argues that far from simply being victims, Africans very much held their own in the balance of power in the Atlantic in the era of the slave trade, controlling the terms of trade and dominating exchanges on the West African coast.

This argument has been controversial. Not because of the issue of Africans selling other Africans: there is no doubt that with only a few partial exceptions, notably Portuguese Angola, Europeans were restricted to the coast throughout the history of the trade, purchasing their slaves from powerful African middlemen. Indeed, slave testimonies reveal that it was common for captives to pass through the hands of multiple owners as they moved down the elaborate commercial networks to the grim barracoons and dungeons of the coastal ports. Here we can see the most obvious historical example of Bayart's concept of 'extraversion': of powerful African states and individuals forging economic links with outside forces by exploiting weaker peoples around them. Rather, the problem is that by stressing African agency, it becomes all too easy to lose sight of the fact that the majority of Africans involved in the making of the Atlantic world *were* victims.

Africa's 'extraversion', moreover, can be exaggerated. Historians have been drawn to the slave trade because of its horrors, its moral implications, its importance in forging an interconnected modern world – and, it must be pointed out, because of the relative abundance of written sources documenting its operation. It has been described with good reason as Africa's 'holocaust', and like the Nazi holocaust of the 1930s–40s, occupies a prominent place in popular perceptions of the past. But, as in the case of the Nazis, there is an argument that it may have been given too much prominence. At certain times, in certain regions, slave raiding had a devastating impact on local communities. Elsewhere, it was an important factor in the accumulation of political and economic power by state-builders and warlords. But it is important that it should not overshadow other historical processes – both 'local' and 'global' – that continued to shape the rhythms of life throughout the continent.

The travels of Mahommah Gardo Baquaqua: Africa and its diaspora

In 1854, a pamphlet entitled *An Interesting Narrative. Biography of Mahommah G. Baquaqua, A Native of Zoogoo, in the Interior of Africa* was published in Detroit, Michigan. In part an abolitionist tract, in part missionary propaganda, it was one of a number of narratives by or about former slaves that appeared in the USA in the years leading up to the Civil War. All of the others, however, concerned slaves born in America. Some accounts exist of the experiences within Africa of 'recaptives'; that is, slaves freed from ships intercepted by British naval patrols and resettled in Sierra Leone, Liberia, and elsewhere. But Baquaqua's narrative is one of just a handful by Africans who actually endured the Middle Passage. The most famous is that of Olaudah Equiano, published in London in 1789 (although recent research has raised serious doubts over the authenticity of Equiano's African birth). Baquaqua's biography, moreover, is unique in being the only known narrative of an African enslaved in Brazil, the destination for one-third of all slaves transported across the Atlantic.

Compiled and edited by an Irish abolitionist churchman, Samuel Moore, it tells an extraordinary story. Mahommah Gardo Baquaqua was born, probably in the late 1820s, in Djougou, a trading town located in the north of modern Bénin. The son of well-off Muslim merchants, he attended Qur'anic school and as a young man secured a position within the household of the local ruler. In about 1845, however, he was kidnapped (by jealous rivals, he claims) and sold into slavery, passing down through the kingdom of Dahomey to the slave-trading port of Ouidah. From there, he was exported to Brazil, where he was the slave of a baker in Pernambuco and then of a ship captain in Rio de Janeiro. On a voyage to New York City in 1847, he managed to escape, subsequently travelling to the black-ruled republic of Haiti. There he became associated with the American Baptist Free Mission, and in 1848 renounced his Muslim upbringing and converted to Christianity. Moving back to the USA and then on to Canada, Baquaqua appears to have produced his biography in the hope of raising funds to enable him to return to Africa as a Christian missionary. His pamphlet, however, made little impact. Thwarted, he sailed for Liverpool, where, in 1857, he disappears from the historical record.

Aside from the fact that it has come down to us at all, Baquaqua's biography is unusual. Very few victims of the transatlantic slave trade would have escaped slavery and gone on to experience that degree of mobility. Yet as a story of bondage and redemption, of physical and spiritual movement that spans Africa, the Americas, and Europe, it encapsulates the essence of the African diaspora. We have already touched on the role of people of African descent in the Americas in shaping both the idea of Africa and of particular identities such as Yoruba. We return to it here in the broader context of the interconnections between African history and the history of the African diaspora. Where does one end and the other begin? How 'African' is the diaspora?

These have long been controversial questions – although more so in America than in Africa. As we have seen, early African American intellectuals envisaged the cultural unity of 'the Negro race'. So too did 20th-century pan-Africanist leaders like W. E. B. Du Bois and Marcus Garvey, the writers of the *négritude* movement, and the anthropologist Melville Herskovits, whose influential *Myth of the Negro Past* (1941) argued for the continuity of African culture amongst the black populations of the Americas. After the Second World War, however, the racial categorization of the world and pan-Africanism as a political

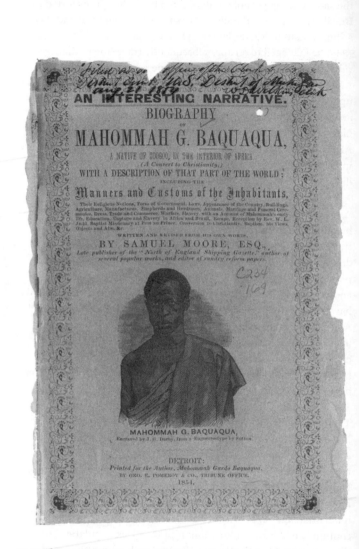

AN INTERESTING NARRATIVE.

BIOGRAPHY

OF

MAHOMMAH G. BAQUAQUA,

A NATIVE OF ZOOGOO, IN THE INTERIOR OF AFRICA

(A Convert to Christianity,)

WITH A DESCRIPTION OF THAT PART OF THE WORLD;

INCLUDING THE

Manners and Customs of the Inhabitants,

Their Religious Notions, Forms of Government, Laws, Appearance of the Country, Buildings, Agriculture, Manufactures, Shepherds and Herdmen, Animals, Marriage and Funeral Ceremonies, Dress, Trade and Commerce, Warfare, Slavery, with an Account of Mahommah's early life, Education, Capture and Slavery in Africa and Brazil, Escape, Reception by Rev. W. L. Judd, Baptist Missionary at Port au Prince, Conversion to Christianity, Baptism, his Views, Objects and Aim, &c.

WRITTEN AND REVISED FROM HIS OWN WORDS,

BY SAMUEL MOORE, ESQ.,

Late publisher of the "North of England Shipping Gazette," author of several popular works, and editor of sundry reform papers.

C234
169

MAHOMMAH G. BAQUAQUA,
Engraved by J. H. Darby, from a Daguerreotype by Sutton

DETROIT:
Printed for the Author, Mahommah Gardo Baquaqua,
BY GEO. E. POMEROY & CO., TRIBUNE OFFICE.
1854.

---

15. Title page of *Biography of Mahommah G. Baquaqua* (Detroit, 1854)

programme both declined. As Patrick Manning points out, it is notable that Du Bois replaced his earlier survey of black history, *The Negro* (1915), with a new version entitled *The World and Africa* (1946). With the rise of African nationalism in the 1950s – and with it the study of African history – the continent itself came into sharper focus. In Manning's words, 'place superseded race'. The history of Africa went one way, and that of the black diaspora the other.

In recent decades, the study of the connections between the two have come very much to the fore. Rather than being concerned with racial essences or with the old debate about the loss or retention of African traits (or 'survivals') in the Americas, historians are now beginning to explore cross-cultural exchanges in a wide variety of contexts: throughout the Atlantic, in the Indian Ocean, and within Africa itself. As research unearths more and more evidence of movement, of cultural transformation, and of boundary crossing – such as Baquaqua's biography – so the possibilities increase for thinking about Africa not as a continent in isolation, but as an integral part of the modern world. Interest in the pan-Africanist visions of anglophone African American elites has now expanded to include research on topics such as the relationship between Africa and Brazil, including the continuing presence of Islam amongst African-Brazilians and the 19th-century movement of freed slaves back to the west coast of Africa.

There is a growing awareness, too, that the notion of diaspora must include Africa itself. As Pier Larson argues in a recent study of the slave trade in the Merina kingdom of highland Madagascar, the process of enslavement involved not just the removal of victims from the shores of Africa but also widespread displacement, trauma, and cultural change within the continent. Indeed, it is quite likely that more Africans were enslaved and relocated within Africa during the era of the Atlantic trade than were exported, especially as the overseas trade was choked off in the 19th century. With this in mind, the question posed above can be reversed: it is not just a matter of thinking about how 'African' is the diaspora, we also need to consider how 'diasporic' is Africa.

Africa's turbulent 19th century

The 19th century was a time of turbulent change in much of Africa. With regard to the three themes we have already considered, the interconnections between local and global forces were transformed in a variety of ways. Across the sudanic zone from Senegal to Sudan, Islamic reformists emerged to challenge the prevailing status quo, seeking to purify the faith and to build new Muslim states. Christian missionary endeavour also entered a more militant phase, Protestant denominations joining the Catholic Church in the effort to evangelize 'heathens' and to turn back the perceived Muslim tide. Entwined with both of these religious processes was the transformation of slavery and the slave trades. Following Britain's abolition of the slave trade in 1807, the Atlantic trade came to a gradual halt – although not before another three million Africans were transported to the Americas. Yet the century witnessed an expansion of slave exports into the Indian Ocean, as well as of enslavement within the continent. Meanwhile, in the Americas, and in the 'creole' communities of the West African coast, literate African elites, energized by Christianity and by abolitionism, began to reimagine their own identities as well as that of a redeemed Africa.

To these processes can be added a further element in Africa's changing engagement with the world: that of the gradual penetration of European imperialism. In terms of direct political control, the European presence on the continent was minimal until the 'Scramble' of the 1880s–90s. Beyond a handful of coastal enclaves that had emerged as outgrowths of the slave trade, European-ruled territory was limited to Africa's southern and northern extremities: the British outpost of the Cape Colony (to which was later added Natal and the independent Boer republics), and, from 1830, the French colony of Algeria. As the century progressed, however, the political and economic clout of industrializing Europe – meaning by and large that of Britain and, to a lesser extent, France – asserted itself in a variety of ways. These added up to what has been called 'informal imperialism'. 'Informal' it may have been, but it represented a fundamental shift in the balance of power on the coasts of Africa.

A signal of things to come was Napoleon Bonaparte's occupation of Egypt in 1798. French forces remained for only three years (before being ejected by the British), but the ease with which they took control of a core province of the Ottoman empire shook the rulers of Muslim North Africa. In Egypt, the aftermath of the occupation saw the rise to power of Muhammad Ali (1805–48), a soldier of Albanian extraction who embarked on a strategy of modernization in order to counter the growing threat of the West. The French intervention also marked a key moment in the development of European ideas about the 'orient'. Napoleon took with him a large contingent of scientists, whose research marked the beginning of the discipline of Egyptology as well as the European scholarly engagement with Islam. They also made off with a large number of ancient artefacts (including the Rosetta Stone, which allowed the translation of Egyptian hieroglyphs): an early example of imperialism as science – or as cultural plunder.

The increasing intervention of Europe into African affairs is apparent in the anti-slave trade campaign. British ships had carried the largest proportion of Africans across the Atlantic in the 18th century, slave-grown Caribbean sugar making a critical contribution to the national economy. In 1807, however, the abolitionist lobby secured the outlawing of the trade for British subjects. Over subsequent decades, Britain cajoled other slave-trading nations to follow suit, imposing a naval blockade of the West African coast and threatening to do the same to Brazil. By the 1850s, the illegal trade was reduced to a trickle. British motives were shaped by a mixture of economic self-interest and high-minded humanitarianism. For the rulers of the coastal middlemen states, however, what the campaign amounted to was a unilateral embargo on their most important export commodity: people. The subsequent encouragement of non-slave exports (so-called legitimate commerce) also carried the tone of a moral crusade. By the high Victorian period, a combination of 'Christianity, civilization, and commerce' was seen to be the key to the redemption of a benighted continent.

The transition from the slave trade to 'legitimate commerce' unfolded in a variety of ways across the continent. In the coastal region of West Africa, agricultural commodities such as palm oil and groundnuts gradually replaced slave exports, in some areas diffusing wealth amongst small producers and traders. The new commerce was often championed by the literate elites of Sierra Leone, Liberia, the Gold Coast, and elsewhere, who emerged as a new kind of 'broker' between Africa and Europe at the expense of the old slave-trading aristocracies. Elsewhere, such as in Dahomey, the latter adapted to changing conditions, diversifying into palm oil but continuing to smuggle slaves (like Mahommah Baquaqua) past Royal Navy patrols.

Yet slavery within Africa, far from 'withering away' with the end of the Atlantic trade as abolitionists had hoped, expanded. Slave labour once exported to the Americas was now exploited more intensively in Africa – ironically, often as a result of the demand for new commodities. The warfare that accompanied the forging of new Islamic states such as the Sokoto Caliphate (in northern Nigeria) generated huge numbers of 'pagan' captives. Many continued to be marched to the coast for illegal export, but more were settled as agricultural workers. After the abolition of slavery in Brazil in 1888, the Sokoto Caliphate was the world's largest slave society, with perhaps one-third of its population in bondage. In northeast Africa, too, state-building was characterized by the enslavement of pagan peoples, as Muhammad Ali and his successors sought to extend Egyptian rule down the Nile and into the equatorial region of Sudan.

16. 'Legitimate commerce' in the 19th century. A diverse crowd of Indians, Arabs, local Swahilis, and Europeans watch a labourer unload tusks in Zanzibar's ivory market, circa 1890–2

Violence, enslavement, and political struggles were also widespread across much of central, eastern, and southern Africa. Here, the commercial transition was dominated not by agricultural production but by foraged products, especially ivory. Vast elephant herds were decimated as ivory-trading frontiers pushed inexorably from the east and west coasts towards the Congo basin. The possession of guns, together with new sources of mercantile wealth, altered the balance of political power in many regions. Established states, such as the Lunda and Luba kingdoms, were brought low by well-armed intruders or by internal dissent. Elsewhere, new domains arose, such as those forged in the eastern Congo by Swahili ivory and slave traders from Zanzibar. In South Africa and in Algeria, meanwhile, white settler frontiers advanced inland, generating armed violence and increasing levels of dispossession.

These multiple processes would culminate in the closing decades of the century in the European conquest and partition of the continent. In the next chapter, we consider this new phase in Africa's long relationship with the world. But we can conclude from the four themes outlined here that Africans were very much part of world history long before the violent imposition of colonial rule. As everywhere, sometimes this was on their own terms, at other times not.

Chapter 5
Colonialism in Africa

Colonial rule came late to Africa. It was also relatively brief. Unlike Latin America, which fell under Spanish and Portuguese rule in the early 16th century and remained that way for 300 years, Africa was conquered by European imperial powers only in the late 19th and early 20th centuries. By the 1960s, the colonial period was all but over. In many parts of the continent, it lasted barely two generations: Morocco, for example, became a French protectorate in 1912 and was again independent in 1956 – the era of colonial domination now shorter than that of renewed sovereignty. While conducting research in the north of Ghana in the late 1990s, one of the present authors interviewed old men and women who as young children remembered the military campaign that in 1911 brought their communities under British overrule. Forty-six years later, in 1957, the British were gone.

In further contrast with the Americas, whose indigenous peoples suffered catastrophic demographic collapse and in some regions cultural annihilation, most African civilizations were robust enough to survive the experience of colonial conquest largely intact. European rule, underpinned throughout the continent by coercion and racism, was often violent, exploitative, and traumatic. But its impact varied enormously: across time, from region to region and colony to colony, between men and women and young and old, and according to a multitude of social, political, and economic factors that were often shaped as much by Africans themselves as by their colonial masters. For some Africans, colonial rule represented a threat; for others, an opportunity. For many, it was probably both. Reconstructing these complex patterns is one of the greatest challenges facing historians of Africa today.

When the systematic study of the African past began in the 1960s, historians were not particularly interested in the period of colonial rule that was then drawing to a close. They were concerned more to look back to precolonial Africa, to demonstrate that the continent had an authentic history before the imposition of European rule (see Chapter 6). Colonial conquest was viewed as an illegitimate rupture, a digression – too close and, for some, too painful, to yet be 'history'. In one influential formulation, pioneering Nigerian historian Jacob Ade Ajayi described colonialism as an ephemeral 'episode in African history', characterized by a fundamental continuity of indigenous institutions. In the 1950s, after all, the history of colonialism was just about the only African history that there was: a story written by Europeans – often colonial officials themselves – of European endeavour in which Africans barely featured. At the height of the liberation struggles, the imperative was to get rid of colonial rule rather than to analyse it. As Frederick Cooper writes in a recent survey of the shifting fortunes of colonial studies: 'Many students thought that all they needed to know about colonialism was its horrors.'

Half a century on, things have changed. The last 20 years have witnessed an extraordinary expansion of interest in the colonial period. Indeed, one often hears the lament at academic conferences and seminars that precolonial history is now sorely neglected – a worry that appears to be borne out if one examines the contents of the leading African history journals. Part of this shift is due simply to the passage of time: the decline and fall of European empires is now as long ago as the Scramble for Africa was in the 1950s. Colonialism is now very much history, the intervening gap providing historians with two crucial resources: written documents, and time for reflection. It is not simply that the range of sources available to write the history of colonial Africa is so much greater than that for all the centuries before – although that certainly is a factor in attracting research. It is also because an expanding range of theoretical tools and analytical insights have enabled historians to think about colonialism in much more sophisticated ways than before. This is also the case with respect to the Americas, to Asia and, indeed, to the imperial 'metropoles' of Europe itself.

This new thinking can be boiled down to one simple observation: colonialism was not just about what European rulers did or thought, it was also about what Africans (or Asians, or others) did and thought. It is no longer adequate to dismiss colonial rule either as a digression from an authentically 'African' history or simply as morally reprehensible. As with the issue of the transatlantic slave trade, historians are as inclined as anybody to hold value judgements about the nature of European imperialism. But their task is to move beyond such judgements in order to reconstruct the lived experience of African peoples under colonial rule in all its complexities and contradictions.

Where Ajayi was right was in his suggestion that imperial power was not as dominant, as coherent, or as monolithic as it tried to pretend. As more becomes known about the myriad ways that Africans actively participated in making the world of colonialism, so too the notion of a distinct 'colonial period' itself becomes problematic. Rather than thinking about the continent's past as a sequence of distinct precolonial, colonial, and postcolonial periods, historians are increasingly concerned to trace patterns of continuity and change between all three.

Conquest

In terms of popular perceptions of the past, both within Africa and beyond, the European 'Scramble' for territory at the end of the 19th century is perhaps the best-known episode in the continent's entire history. Ironically, it also remains one of the least understood. Part of the problem is that colonial conquest has often been seen more as an event of European history rather than of African history: a drama of imperial rivalries, high diplomacy, and audacious military feats played out on a vast continental stage where Africans have few speaking parts. Moreover, while it is useful in some respects to see the conquest as a scramble, it was also a series of regional *scrambles*, plural, unfolding for different reasons in different parts of the continent.

Historical debates about these reasons have turned on a range of intersecting issues: whether the roots of partition lie in Europe or in Africa; the extent to which economic motives were the key factor; whether the shift to territorial conquest represented a distinctly new type of imperialism or continuity from older forms of informal control. These questions began to emerge in Europe while the conquest was still underway, when the British liberal writer J. A. Hobson argued that the South African (or 'Boer') War of 1899–1902 was being waged in order that British-based capitalists could secure control over the region's gold mines. They have faded from view somewhat in recent years, as historians, suspicious of monocausal explanations and grand 'metanarratives', have turned to exploring the multitude of discordant voices, both European and African, that arose from the experience of colonial conquest.

Amidst all this debate, let's start with some key facts. In the final quarter of the 19th century, the gradual European penetration of Africa suddenly accelerated into a head-long rush for territorial conquest. The imperial powers involved were those with established commercial interests and coastal enclaves, Britain, France, and Portugal (the latter dating back to the 16th century), and a group who hitherto had had little or nothing to do with the continent, Germany, Italy, and, as a private colonial entrepreneur, King Leopold of Belgium. A seventh European state, the waning imperial power of Spain, also secured a few small territories.

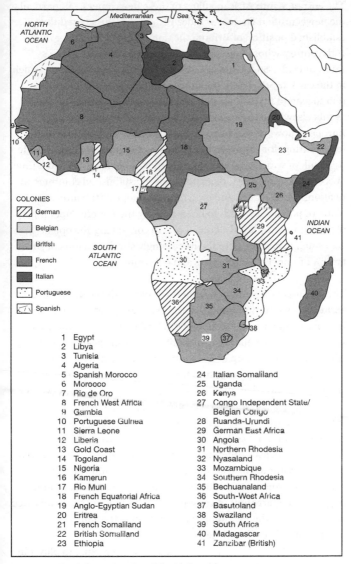

COLONIES

- ▨ German
- ▨ Belgian
- ▨ British
- ▨ French
- ▨ Italian
- ⣿ Portuguese
- ▨ Spanish

1 Egypt
2 Libya
3 Tunisia
4 Algeria
5 Spanish Morocco
6 Morocco
7 Rio de Oro
8 French West Africa
9 Gambia
10 Portuguese Guinea
11 Sierra Leone
12 Liberia
13 Gold Coast
14 Togoland
15 Nigeria
16 Kamerun
17 Rio Muni
18 French Equatorial Africa
19 Anglo-Egyptian Sudan
20 Eritrea
21 French Somaliland
22 British Somaliland
23 Ethiopia
24 Italian Somaliland
25 Uganda
26 Kenya
27 Congo Independent State/
   Belgian Congo
28 Ruanda-Urundi
29 German East Africa
30 Angola
31 Northern Rhodesia
32 Nyasaland
33 Mozambique
34 Southern Rhodesia
35 Bechuanaland
36 South-West Africa
37 Basutoland
38 Swaziland
39 South Africa
40 Madagascar
41 Zanzibar (British)

Map 4. Colonial empires in Africa before 1914

The entrance into African affairs of these newcomers – in particular the newly unified Germany under Bismarck – threatened the established position of Britain, the dominant world power in the 19th century whose merchants controlled the bulk of Africa's external trade. So too did the new 'forward policy' of France, which in the early 1880s gave its military commanders in Senegal free rein to extend territorial control inland while encouraging its agents elsewhere to secure treaties with local rulers. For the European powers, the value of African trade was small, representing, for example, less than 5% of Britain's overseas trade (the bulk of which was with Egypt and South Africa). But at a time of economic downturn, rising tensions in established commercial relations on the coast, and growing knowledge of the interior, the allure of potential wealth to be secured by the forceful 'opening up' of the continent played a crucial role in convincing European statesmen to acquiesce to the increasingly shrill demands of small groups of imperial enthusiasts and opportunists.

The speculative nature of conquest is clear, with the desire to exclude rivals from potentially lucrative regions often being more important than the protection of established interests. But there was also a strong collaborative strain in the European carve-up of Africa. The opening up of the continent was regarded as an ennobling 'mission', not just to trade with, but through doing so to civilize a backward, benighted people. Imperialist rhetoric was a heady mix of self-interest, racial arrogance, and missionary zeal – similar in many ways to that of the earlier anti-slave trade campaign. Imperial collaboration was also apparent in the famous Berlin West Africa Conference of 1884–5, which served to sort out existing territorial contests and to lay down ground rules for subsequent annexations. The rules of the game worked, by and large. The demarcation of coastal spheres of influence was followed in the 1890s by the headlong race to establish the 'effective occupation' of interior hinterlands. For all the popular jingoism and sabre rattling, no two European powers ever came to blows in Africa – until, that is, the First World War.

That, in a nutshell, is the European side of the story. The reality of conquest as it unfolded on the ground was, of course, a lot more complex. For a start, the avoidance of violence between imperial rivals did not extend to their African opponents. Occupation was often secured by negotiation and treaty, with dubious offers of 'protection' (and it was very much in the mafia sense of the term) being extended to local rulers. But in many regions European forces faced stiff resistance – often after intense debates within African states and communities on how best to defend local sovereignty. Armed resistance tended to come either from militarized states, many of which had built up their own coercive capabilities earlier in the turbulent 19th century, or from stubbornly independent stateless peoples for whom any sort of overrule was anathema.

In the face of the overwhelming superiority of European industrial technology, however, resistance proved to be futile. It is notable that when France invaded Algiers in 1830, it enjoyed little or no advantage in weapons technology and became embroiled in a costly 17-year war of attrition against local forces that tied down large numbers of metropolitan troops. By the end of the century, in contrast, the 'tools of empire' brutally swept aside Africa's warrior elites. These tools were not just guns, but medicines, steamships, railways, telegraphs, and the organizational capabilities of the industrial state. Yet it was the technology gap in weaponry that was crucial – horrifically illustrated at the battle of Omdurman in 1898, when the Sudanese Mahdist soldiers repeatedly charged Kitchener's machine guns, leaving some 11,000 dead for the loss of 49 soldiers on the British side.

Conquest was further facilitated – and, importantly, cheapened – by the widespread use of locally recruited African soldiers. Many were ex-slaves who had much to gain from the overthrow of the established order. An early model for such mercenary forces were the *tirailleurs sénégalais*, the 'Senegalese Riflemen', who fought their way across the sudanic zone of West Africa in the service of France. Only two sets of African state-builders came close to

17. Conquest. The Mahdist commander Mahmud Ibn Ahmad (whose signature appears in Arabic) held by soldiers of the 10th Sudanese Battalion following his capture at the Battle of Atbara during the Anglo-Egyptian conquest of the Sudan in 1898. Mahmud wears the *jibba*, the appliquéd smock of the *Ansar*, the warriors of the Mahdist movement

matching the political and military resources of their European rivals: the white Boer republics of South Africa and the rulers of the ancient highland kingdom of Ethiopia. The former held out against the might of the British empire for three years, finally surrendering after a bitter and costly war in 1902. Ethiopia alone won the race for power, routing an invading Italian army in 1896, securing its sovereignty by treaty, and going on to extend its own imperial rule over surrounding peoples. It would remain independent until 1936, when it fell to Mussolini's invading fascist army. By then, the arms gap had increased further, Emperor Haile Sellassie's cavalry succumbing to Italian armour, aeroplanes, and poison gas.

Despite the speed of partition, the process of colonial conquest continued in some regions for many decades. Once Morocco had fallen under French rule and Libya under Italian rule in 1912, the entire continent with the exception of Ethiopia and the African American settler state of Liberia had, on paper, been incorporated into European empires. Yet colonial armies and bureaucracies were tiny, and huge swathes of territory remained outside any effective control. The conquest of stateless peoples in the forests of West Africa and across the sudanic zone, for example, was prolonged, characterized by brutal punitive expeditions that targeted entire communities.

Other peoples rose in rebellion against the oppressive demands of the early colonial state, notably the Ndebele of Southern Rhodesia in 1896, the Asante of the Gold Coast in 1900, and the Herero of German South West Africa in 1904 (now Zimbabwe, Ghana, and Namibia, respectively). Perhaps the best-known uprising against colonial rule was the Maji Maji rebellion in German East Africa (now Tanzania) in 1905–7, which united diverse peoples under the banner of a religious movement that distributed sacred water, or *maji*, as protection from German bullets. As amongst the Herero, the loss of life in the resulting suppression and subsequent famine was enormous. The devastated region had barely begun to recover when it was engulfed by the allied campaign against German forces in the First World War.

The most devastating social disruption and loss of life in early colonial Africa, however, took place in King Leopold's so-called Congo Independent State. Here violence was associated not with the suppression of rebellion but with a desperate attempt to extract wealth in the form of ivory and rubber from the scattered populations of the equatorial forest. This was the setting of Joseph Conrad's *Heart of Darkness* (1901) and his scathing short story, *An Outpost of Progress* (1897). The effort by missionaries and journalists to alert the world to the atrocities in the Congo can be seen as the first successful human rights campaign of the 20th century. In 1908, Leopold was forced by international pressure to hand his vast private fiefdom over to the Belgian government.

The First World War was, with the exception of the Italian invasion of Ethiopia, the final act in the partition of Africa. Following its defeat in 1918, Germany lost its colonial possessions, which were divided amongst the victorious allies, technically as 'mandates' under the oversight of the new League of Nations. The victors included the Union of South Africa, from 1910 a self-governing Dominion of the British empire that emerged as a sub-imperial power in its own right when it was granted the mandate over neighbouring South West Africa. The multilayered nature of 'sub-imperialism' was also evident in the Sudan, which after its reconquest from the Mahdist regime was governed jointly by Britain and its protectorate, Egypt. The aftermath of war witnessed a further reorganization of empire, when a resurgence of Egyptian nationalism forced Britain to grant the country semi-independence in 1922. Egypt and South Africa were exceptional cases. After the violence of the era of conquest, by the interwar period European rule seemed secure throughout tropical Africa. But the overlapping chronology is telling: no sooner had the final imperial map of Africa taken shape than the first signs of an unravelling of colonialism began to appear.

Colonial states

How did the European powers rule their new African empires? What exactly is meant by 'colonialism' in the African context? In considering these questions, it is important to stress that little systematic thought was given to how African possessions should be run. What thought there was, moreover, rarely made it off the drawing board – and that which did tended to dissipate when rulers were confronted with the stark realities of administering vast tracts of territory and diverse, often recalcitrant peoples on shoestring budgets. The speed of partition meant that colonial states were improvised affairs from the outset, based on a variety of *ad hoc* arrangements determined largely by local conditions. Ideas about how best to manage 'natives' were often transferred from previous colonial encounters: in the case of Britain, from its Indian empire, and France, from its North African bridgehead in Algeria. But such ideas were often contested and contradictory. French officialdom, for example, displayed an ambivalent attitude towards Islam: Muslims were generally regarded as superior in terms of civilization to 'pagan' peoples, but were also seen to be inherently disloyal.

Early on at least, there were some differences in national 'styles' of rule. The officials of republican France were often quick to dismantle uncooperative African ruling structures, in line with a vague ideology that sought ultimately to transform indigenous society by 'assimilating' it to metropolitan culture. At the heart of the notion of assimilation was the distinction between citizen and subject, the latter being subject to the harsh terms of the 'native' legal code, the *indigénat* (versions of which were also operated by the Portuguese and Belgians). British officials, in contrast, were more inclined to make use of existing rulers – especially if, as in the case of the emirs of the Sokoto Caliphate of northern Nigeria, the latter were aristocratic authoritarians with whom business could be done.

It was this more conservative model, as pioneered in northern

Nigeria by Lord Lugard, that came to be known as 'indirect rule'. By the time of the Depression of the 1930s, when cost-efficiency was the order of the day, it had been adopted in one shape or another throughout the continent by all the colonial powers. European imperialists invaded Africa on the pretext that Africans were incapable of properly governing themselves; once established there, however, they found they were unable to govern without the participation of African allies and intermediaries.

As has been the case in empires throughout history, many Africans chose to embrace the new colonial order and worked to turn it to their own advantage. Such individuals ranged from humble ex-slaves who enrolled in colonial armies, clerks and interpreters who used literacy as an avenue of social and economic advance, on to kings and chiefs who consolidated their political positions in alliance with European power. Of the latter, one of the most famous was Sir Apolo Kaggwa (1869–1927), who played a key role in negotiating British overrule in the Buganda kingdom in modern Uganda. Christian missionaries had a significant impact in Buganda in the 1880s, attracting ambitious young men whose newly found literacy earned them the status of 'reader'. By the end of the decade, as rival Muslim, Protestant, and Catholic factions vied for power at the royal court, the young Kaggwa became leader of the Protestants, forging an alliance with incoming British forces and, with their backing, becoming *katikiro* or 'prime minister'.

With the encouragement of missionary-ethnographer John Roscoe, Kaggwa began collecting oral traditions. In 1901, he published *Basekabaka be Buganda* ('The Kings of Buganda'), the first of three works in Luganda on the history and customs of his people. Kaggwa emerges as the archetypal modernizer and 'cultural broker', skilfully mediating between colonial power and indigenous culture. His books – which he published himself on his own printing press – represent the earliest recension of the royal history of Buganda. Like Johnson's *History of the Yorubas*, Kaggwa's work was, of course, a particular version of history. It too prompted a succession of responses, written by the literate representatives of neighbouring kingdoms such as Buganda's long-standing rival, Bunyoro. Modern historians regard such early written histories as complex primary sources, needing careful contextualization in the power structures from which they emerged. For many Ugandans, however, Kaggwa's books have come to represent *the* 'official' version of the Bugandan past. His influence as a cultural broker very much continues today.

Such African allies were critical for a simple reason: colonial rule in Africa was done on the cheap. This was as true for imperial Britain as it was for impoverished and backward Portugal. The grand visions and wildly inflated hopes of untapped wealth quickly faded, replaced by an ongoing struggle on the part of thinly stretched bureaucracies to impose law and order, to raise taxes, and to mobilize labour. The resulting economic systems were as diverse as those of the precolonial past – and in many regions were based on the commercial transformations of the 19th century. Where African farmers had already forged viable export economies, notably in Egypt and in the coastal and forest zones of West Africa, colonial states were eager for them to continue to expand commodity production. Remote, less fertile hinterland regions such as the sudanic zone of French West Africa, in contrast, were often subjected to more coercive revenue-extraction measures: punishing levels of head-tax, forced labour (extracted under the terms of the *indigénat*), and compulsory cultivation.

Coercion also characterized much of French- and Belgian-ruled equatorial Africa and Portuguese-ruled Angola and Mozambique. In the equatorial forest region in particular, the early colonial state was so under-resourced that it farmed out control over vast tracts of territory to so-called concessionary companies, smash-and-grab outfits whose main concern was to pillage as much wealth as quickly as possible. Just as West Africa's peasant farming systems were founded on precolonial initiatives, so too can the concessionary regimes be seen as a continuation of the crude violence of the slave and ivory raiding frontiers that swept into the

18. Cultural brokers. Apolo Kaggwa, *katikiro* of Buganda (right), poses with his friend and fellow Christian modernizer Ham Mukasa in 1902. Photograph by Sir Benjamin Stone

Congo basin in the 19th century. This was the state as predator, personified by the peoples of the lower Congo River as *bula matari*, the 'breaker of rocks'. The destruction was such that Jan Vansina has argued, in sharp contrast to Jacob Ajayi's view of the colonial period, that conquest spelt the 'death of the old tradition' throughout equatorial Central Africa. These two contrasting historical perspectives speak volumes about the huge regional diversity of the colonial experience.

Elsewhere, notably in French North Africa and in British-ruled Kenya, Southern Rhodesia and, until 1910, South Africa, officials believed that the chief agents of economic advance should be white settlers rather than African producers. In these regions, 'colonialism' meant something quite different again. European communities remained small minorities everywhere, including in the two great outposts of white settlement at either end of the continent, Algeria and South Africa. But settlers had a disproportionate, albeit contested, influence on the trajectory of

19. **Work and mobility. Laying railway tracks in the Belgian Congo in 1914**

economic and social change in their respective colonies. For indigenous African populations, this influence tended to be detrimental: settlers were usually allocated the best agricultural land, whose previous guardians were reduced to being landless labourers or were forced into overcrowded 'native reserves'. In British East Africa and in South Africa, the situation was further complicated by sizable populations of Indian migrants, who occupied an ambiguous middle tier in the colonial racial hierarchy.

In South Africa, Southern Rhodesia and Northern Rhodesia (now Zambia), and in the southern part of the Belgian Congo, moreover, European mining companies competed with white farmers for access to African labour. Early on, many Africans workers and farmers – especially young men seeking to escape paternal authority – took advantage of the new-found availability of wage labour and the expansion of markets for foodstuffs. By the interwar period, however, the so-called 'settler-mining' economies were becoming increasingly coercive, as land alienation and the demands of migrant labour systems were placing huge strains on many African communities.

All these demands being placed on Africans throughout the continent: to pay taxes, to grow new crops, to move aside for white settlers, to travel to new areas to work, created another contradiction at the heart of colonialism. The overriding European vision of Africa was that it was static, primitive, 'traditional' – a condition that colonial rulers, by and large, believed it was in their own interest and in that of their African subjects to preserve. Yet the exploitation of the continent's natural resources and manpower was creating widespread social change. From north to south, people were being drawn into cash economies, reformulating family relationships, moving to towns and cities, breaking old bonds of allegiance and creating new ones.

Some of these bonds were contained within individual territories, giving rise by the 1930s to an inchoate sense of being, say,

Colonial knowledge

To rule Africa, colonial officials needed knowledge about African languages, cultures, and laws, which in many regions began to be compiled with the assistance of local intermediaries within a few years of occupation. In some cases, this process extended to knowledge of the past, notably with the work of a number of administrator-scholars in French North and West Africa. Historical material on Algeria appeared from as early as 1856 in the *Revue Africaine*, and by 1900, O. Houdas's translation of the *Ta'rikh al-sudan* had been published in Paris. The most prominent figure in this respect was Maurice Delafosse, who in 1909 introduced the teaching of African languages at the École Coloniale in Paris. With Houdas, he translated the other great Timbuktu chronicle, the *Ta'rikh al-fattash*, and in 1912 produced a massive, three-volume survey of the Mande world, *Haut-Sénégal-Niger*, including much historical material derived from the chronicles and from oral sources. A comparable British figure was H. R. Palmer, who immersed himself in indigenous accounts of the history of northern Nigeria. Such works were products of their times – Palmer, for example, was a firm believer in the Hamitic hypothesis – but remind us that the colonial vision of Africa as a continent without history was far from monolithic.

Senegalese, or Nigerian, or Kenyan. Others crossed colonial frontiers, creating linkages and circulating ideas across regions and, for a tiny number of Africans, beyond the shores of the continent itself. Widening networks of belonging ranged from working class affiliation to an identity as African or as a member of the black race. Far more Africans were embracing Islam and Christianity. Many

54 – Afrique Occidentale – SÉNÉGAL – SAINT-LOUIS – Mounment Faidherbe

Collection Générale Fortier, Dakar

20. **Town life.** Passing hawkers or shoppers pose beneath a statue of Louis Faidherbe, the French governor who in the 1850s initiated the conquest of Senegal, in Saint-Louis, Senegal's colonial capital. Photograph by Edmond Fortier, circa 1900

also sought social advance through Western education, often provided at mission schools and therefore associated with the personal liberation of Christian conversion. Educational provision varied hugely – from the non-existent to the barely adequate – and only a few had the opportunity to advance beyond primary level. But widening literacy was a revolutionary change in Africa. To say that African societies survived colonialism, therefore, is not to say that they survived unchanged.

Despotism *versus* ornamentalism: debates about indirect rule

It is only recently that historians have begun to examine in detail the social and the cultural changes of the colonial era in Africa. The result has been a growing awareness of the ability of Africans to continue to shape their own lives, as well as to shape the nature of colonialism itself. The more we discover about colonial rule, the more fragmented, contradictory, and malleable it appears to be, dependent on the active participation of some Africans and full of autonomous spaces within which others pursued their own agendas. No longer are Africans seen as simply 'responding' to the imposition of alien rule by either outright 'resistance' or self-interested 'collaboration'. To borrow the title of David Robinson's study of the relationship between French colonial authorities and Muslim society in Senegal and Mauritania, both rulers and ruled can be seen to have experimented with a variety of 'paths of accommodation' with each other. Coercion and domination, in short, are out; 'accommodation', 'encounter', 'appropriation', and 'African agency' are in.

Like new ways of thinking about the impact of the slave trade, the danger here is that of throwing out the baby with the bathwater: of losing sight of fundamentals in order to embrace new paradigms – or, in some cases, to return to even older ones. Just because colonialism was feeble does not necessarily mean that it was any less coercive. Indeed, the weaker the state, as we have seen in equatorial Africa, the more violent and crudely exploitative it could be. The sheer diversity of the colonial experience across space and time – even within one territory, let alone an entire empire-state – makes historical iconoclasm a risky business.

This is apparent in two recent books by prominent (non-Africanist) historians about the British empire: David Cannadine's *Ornamentalism*, and Niall Ferguson's *Empire*. In *Ornamentalism* (a clever play on words of Edward Said's *Orientalism*), Cannadine argues that the key to understanding imperial rule was not the perceived racial difference between the British ruler and the native 'other', but the mutual class affinity between the British and indigenous hierarchies. Ferguson's *Empire*, while acknowledging the brutality of imperial conquest, argues that the British empire was a positive force in spreading free market capitalism, the rule of law, and democracy – values that many colonial subjects eagerly grasped. Both works make serious points; certainly, neither historian can be accused of being an apologist for imperialism (although some have argued that Ferguson comes close). It is likely, however, that both are at best only partially right. As with older debates on the 'Scramble', great care is needed in order to avoid generic pronouncements on what 'colonial rule' in Africa and elsewhere was really all about.

Far from being settled one way or another, the issues raised by Cannadine and Ferguson with regard to the British empire – the nature of colonial rule; the question of what colonized peoples themselves sought to appropriate from the imperial encounter – continue to be reconstructed and refined by historians of Africa. One set of questions is that regarding the role of Africans in the creation of 'tradition', of 'custom', and of new identities – all within the broad context of the formulation of indirect rule. These issues are of particular relevance to us here because they involved the local production of ethnographic and historical knowledge, such as Johnson's *History of the Yorubas* and Apolo Kaggwa's *Basekabaka be Buganda*. By the interwar period, similar writings were appearing in many parts of the continent, often arising from debates and struggles *within* African societies over control of the past and claims on the present. One famous example is Jomo Kenyatta's *Facing Mount Kenya* (1938), a historical ethnography of the Kikuyu people of Kenya that sought to reconcile conflicting Kikuyu responses to the loss of land and sovereignty to white settlers and the colonial state.

At the heart of the debate is the idea of the 'invention of tradition', a term coined in 1983 by Eric Hobsbawm and Terence Ranger; that is, that supposedly ancient, timeless traditions (not just in Africa, but in Europe and elsewhere) are often nothing of the sort, but are recent creations designed to legitimate the exercise of political power. Armed with this insight, many historians detected the influence of missionaries, officials, and ethnographers, in collusion with local intermediaries, in imposing a new, distinctly 'colonial' vision on Africa. As we have seen in Chapter 2, this vision saw African society as comprising a series of distinct tribes. It was these tribes, each with its own set of traditions, customs, and laws, and each with its own 'chiefs' whose authority was backed by colonial officials, that formed the building blocks of indirect rule. According to one scholar, Mahmood Mamdani, indirect rule created a series of 'decentralized despotisms', illegitimate power structures that survived the end of colonial rule and that in part explain the political authoritarianism of contemporary Africa. Colonial rulers, in short, set out to preserve African society, but it was an African society of its own making.

These insights have been important in exploring the impact of colonial rule on Africa. But they have in turn been criticized for being overly 'constructivist'; that is, for placing too much emphasis on the ability of colonial power to manipulate local knowledge and on the gullibility of Africans in accepting invented traditions. 'Traditions', it has been argued, are more complex than that: they needed at least some historical basis and legitimacy, or they simply would not have worked as instruments of rule. Mamdani's thesis of

111

21. Indirect rulers. King Njoya of Bamum (in present-day Cameroon), sitting on his beaded throne at his capital Foumban with members of his court and the Austrian trader Rudolf Oldenburg. A tireless innovator and modernizer, Njoya (reigned 1885–1933) oversaw the invention of a new religion combining Islam, Christianity, and indigenous practices, a new language developed from German, French, and the vernacular, and an ideographic script in which to record his kingdom's history, law, and customs. Photograph by Helga Oldenburg, c. 1912

'decentralized despotism', for example, can be criticized for its underestimation of the multiplying social links noted above, links that cut across indirect rule chieftaincies. As we have seen with the 19th-century emergence of Yoruba and Zulu identity, these processes were often underway well before the imposition of colonial rule. And by the 1930s, even the best-off colonial states had become holding operations, singularly ill-equipped to contain or to understand the changes they had unleashed.

The debate goes on, and the idea of the 'invention' will be further refined as more becomes known about the agency of Africans themselves in imagining and re-imagining notions of tradition, identity, and power.

Chapter 6
Imagining the future, rebuilding the past

The two decades following the Second World War were a time of dramatic change for Africa. The tensions and contradictions of colonial empire that had become apparent by the 1930s came to a head after 1945, as European rulers struggled to contain the aspirations of their African subjects. Having barely managed to consolidate itself in the interwar period, the colonial state buckled and then collapsed under the combined weight of the cost of economic development and the escalating demand for political freedoms. The two most important powers, Britain and France, attempted to control change by creating reformed, more inclusive colonial systems. But local politicians and their followers began to imagine a future free of the injustices and frustrations of colonial rule, a future of self-governed nations that could guarantee economic and social advance into the modern world.

Reformist plans were swept aside by the rising tide of African expectations. In 1945, only four African countries, Ethiopia (liberated from Italian rule in 1941), Liberia, Egypt, and South Africa, were independent – although Egypt remained a British protectorate in all but name and South Africa was governed by a white minority regime. By the mid-1950s, all of North Africa except Algeria was independent and by the mid-1960s most of tropical Africa had followed. With the exception of the intransigent Portuguese empire and the white supremacist states of the south, where wars of liberation dragged on into the last quarter of the century, Africa's 'postcolonial' period had begun.

It is no coincidence that the era of anti-colonial nationalism and liberation was also that of the emergence of African history as an academic discipline. If the rapidly changing postwar landscape demanded new ways of envisaging contemporary African society and of imagining its future, it also entailed a revolution in ways of looking at the past. Western education and literacy had transformed African society and politics, and it was in the universities established in the terminal phase of colonial rule as well as in those of Europe and North America that a new generation of professionally trained historians began the task of reconstructing the continent's history.

Like colonial rule itself, there has been much debate over the dynamics of decolonization in Africa. Did the transfer of power to nationalist leaders represent a real watershed, the winning back of indigenous sovereignty and the start of a new era of political freedom? Or was the process characterized more by continuity, by the replacement of one set of autocratic rulers by another in a seamless transition from colony to 'postcolony'? These debates continue – and as the archival records of the postwar period become available, involve increasing numbers of historians. There can be no doubt, however, about the fundamental transformation in perceptions of the continent's past. Whereas European knowledge had long denied Africans a history, the second half of the 20th century has seen that history break down the doors of the Western academy. And from the very outset, the project of rebuilding the African past was linked to imagining a new African future.

Africa's postwar moment

From our vantage point at the beginning of the 21st century, it is tempting to see the collapse of European-ruled colonial empires as inevitable. But this was not how things necessarily looked to Africans in the 1940s and 1950s. For many, the bonds of empire appeared to be tightening rather than loosening. In a continuation of wartime central planning and efforts to raise commodity production and to mobilize labour, colonial states became increasingly ambitious, 'developmentalist', and intrusive into everyday life. The impact of what has been called the 'second colonial occupation' was complex: widening opportunity and the expansion of health, educational, and welfare provision for many Africans – admittedly, often from a very low base – but also growing unrest on the part of both peasant farmers and urban workers.

Labour militancy had begun to emerge in some regions during the Depression, resulting in a major strike in the Northern Rhodesian copper mines in 1935. Unrest continued in many colonies through the war, culminating in a series of stoppages in the mid-1940s: notably on the South African gold mines in 1946; general strikes in the cities of Dakar in 1946, and Mombasa and Dar es Salaam in 1947; in Southern Rhodesia in 1948; and, most dramatically, the five-month strike on the railways of French West Africa in 1947–8. As improving healthcare and fertility levels led to accelerating population growth, migrants from the countryside flooded into cities all over the continent. Despite attempts in 'settler Africa' to control the migrant labour system and the ideology of indirect rule that perceived African society essentially as rural, tribal, and traditional, it was the rapidly growing cities that emerged as the key crucibles of change and where colonial rulers began to lose their tenuous grip on power.

The Second World War was a turning point, but as Frederick Cooper shows in his recent book on Africa since 1940, the political direction the continent would take was far from clear. France, keen to reassert control over its empire following the trauma of wartime defeat, from 1944 fashioned a new constitutional relationship with its colonies, one that for the first time emphasized economic and social progress but that affirmed the unity of the 'French Union'.

22. Higher education. A student working in the library of Yaba College in Lagos, Nigeria, in 1947

Elections based on a gradually widening franchise carried African representatives to parliament in Paris, including Léopold Senghor, the Senegalese poet and co-founder of the *négritude* movement, and Félix Houphouët-Boigny, a doctor and champion of African cocoa farmers in Côte d'Ivoire. In 1946, Houphouët-Boigny introduced the legislation that finally ended forced labour in the French empire, while the Senegalese lawyer Lamine Guèye initiated that which ended the legal distinction between citizen and subject. Free finally from the hated *indigénat*, the inhabitants of France's vast domains in North, West, and Equatorial Africa and on the island of Madagascar were all now 'citizens'. But they were citizens of a centralized and reinvigorated Greater France. When a peasant rebellion in Madagascar in 1947 threatened French rule, the response was brutal. Perhaps 100,000 Malagasy died in the counter-insurgency campaign – a bloody reminder of the era of colonial conquest and a presage of the wars of liberation to come.

Despite the loss of its Indian empire in 1947, Britain too was eager to reclaim great power status and to mobilize colonial production in order to rebuild its shattered economy. It took a different and initially more hesitant route to constitutional reform than France, laying plans to expand African representation in local legislatures and to turn the imploding system of indirect rule into more democratic 'local government'. Yet it was events in Africa that would force the pace of change. In February 1948, the Gold Coast, long recognized as Britain's 'model' African colony, was shaken by an outbreak of urban rioting that derailed plans for strictly limited reform. Following the recommendations of a commission of inquiry – that very British response to a political crisis – the Colonial Office in London committed itself to a path that would result in self-government for the Gold Coast. The political initiative was quickly seized by the radical anti-colonial firebrand Kwame Nkrumah, who broke from the more established and elitist African politicians to found his own mass nationalist party. By 1951, the charismatic Nkrumah had been elected 'Leader of Government Business' (effectively prime minister), his clarion call for full independence an inspiration for emerging nationalists across Africa.

In a pattern that would recur throughout the continent in subsequent years, the rulers of the Gold Coast had in a moment of crisis surrendered control over the process of political reform. Concessions were met with more demands. In the context of the emerging Cold War, the imperative for the colonial powers was to identify and to cultivate 'moderate' African partners in order to head off more radical alternatives. Where the latter posed a direct challenge to colonial control, as in Madagascar in 1947 and in subsequent armed uprisings in Kenya in 1952–6 (the 'Mau Mau rebellion'), Cameroon in 1956–8, and Algeria in 1954–62, the result was fierce repression. Regarded by European rulers and settlers as an outburst of irrational violence on the part of confused, 'detribalized' Africans, the Mau Mau uprising has been analysed with great sophistication by historians of Kenya. A conflict once

23. Negotiated decolonization. Casting a ballot in Accra in the Gold Coast elections of 1951 (present-day Ghana), which resulted in a landslide victory for Kwame Nkrumah's Convention People's Party. A British colonial public relations photograph labelled 'Miss Mensah goes to vote'

seen as inexplicable now occupies a prominent place in the historiography of decolonization.

African politicians of all hues, meanwhile, needed to establish their own popular legitimacy. In common with an earlier generation of Asian nationalists, most were urban-based, Western-educated, 'middle-class' figures, from social groups who had benefited from the opportunities of the colonial period. Their task was to 'capture the countryside', that is, to convince the mass of newly enfranchised rural voters that the future lay with them rather than with the established indirect rule 'chiefs'. A few, like Léopold Senghor in Senegal and Milton Margai in Sierra Leone, were representatives at the outset of rural interests and whose political goal was therefore to oust established urban elites. Far from being a simple two-way contest between European proconsuls on the one hand and nationalist liberators on the other, the decolonization process was also a mosaic of political struggles *within* African society.

If the Gold Coast riots in 1948 represented a symbolic turning point in West Africa, then the victory of the National Party in whites-only elections in South Africa the same year indicated a different trajectory for much of southern and central Africa. The National Party, the vehicle of a renewed Afrikaner nationalism, set about entrenching racial segregation and white economic power in South Africa under the slogan of 'apartheid', literally 'separateness'. Determined to turn the tide on black urbanization, the increasingly oppressive apartheid state can be seen as representing the final, monstrous manifestation of a colonial migrant labour system that sought to exploit 'traditional' rural Africa. The South African model appealed to the smaller settler communities of the Rhodesias and Kenya, which also emerged from the war strengthened and ready to press their claims for white-dominated self-government.

In the Portuguese colonies of Angola and Mozambique and in the mining region of southern Belgian Congo, settler populations and expatriate mining concerns were also expanding rapidly. As late as

24. Anti-colonial protest and white power. Demonstrators in Salisbury (now Harare) confront armed police following the outlawing of the Zimbabwe African People's Union (ZAPU) in Southern Rhodesia (Zimbabwe) on 20 September 1962

1957, the paternalistic rulers of the Congo believed self-government to be generations away, while the rightist dictatorship in Portugal had no intention to extend democratic rights to its own people let alone those of its African empire. As much of North and West Africa embarked on the path to constitutional reform, white settler power to the south appeared to be entering a new period of ascendancy. Here, decolonization was often protracted and violent, characterized by rural insurgency rather than urban negotiation. Algeria, too, with its one million European settlers, experienced a bitter liberation war between 1954 and 1962, a conflict that traumatized both colonized and colonizer and which in its latter stages threatened to spill over into metropolitan France itself.

The decolonization of African history

It was this heady climate of social change, soaring expectation, and political struggle that fertilized the seeds of scholarly research into Africa's history. The crucial breeding grounds for this intellectual endeavour were the institutions of higher learning established as part of the expansion of education in British West Africa, together with a handful of pioneering university departments in Britain and the United States. Again, 1948 was a key year, with the foundation of the university colleges of Ibadan in Nigeria and the Gold Coast (at Legon, on the outskirts of Accra), the creation at Northwestern University (at Evanston, near Chicago) of the first interdisciplinary African studies programme in North America, and the appointment of Roland Oliver as the first lecturer in the history of Africa at the School of Oriental and African Studies in London (Oliver and his colleague John Fage subsequently founded the *Journal of African History* and co-wrote the first modern textbook on the history of the continent). By 1951, Uganda and Sudan also had new universities, as did independent Ethiopia.

The process of shaking off the legacy of colonial historiography, however, would be long, arduous, and much contested. 'History' at the new African universities still meant essentially European

25. Anti-colonial war memorialized in cinema. A still from Gillo
Pontecorvo's 1965 film *The Battle of Algiers*, which reconstructed the
bitter struggle in 1957 between FLN nationalist fighters and French
paratroopers to control the casbah in the heart of the Algerian capital.
The film, shot on location, was written and co-produced by ex-FLN
commander Saadi Yacef, who also played himself on screen

history, as Nigerian historian Jacob Ajayi remembered of the degree offered from 1949 at University College, Ibadan. The closest students got to studying their own past was a course titled 'The History of European Activities in Africa', the main text for which was *The Colonization of Africa by Alien Races* by the pioneering linguist and colonial official Harry Johnson, published in 1899! This book, Ajayi recalled, 'was regarded as the most scholarly single volume available on African history', and although it was gradually supplemented with new material, the course itself remained on the books until Ibadan ended its affiliation with the University of London in 1962.

Just as the Gold Coast, and in its wake, Nigeria, were at the forefront of the negotiated path to independence, so too did their flagship universities lead the way in the project of decolonizing the African past. The University of Ibadan in particular became emblematic of the first, so-called 'nationalist' wave of African historiography, that developed in tandem with the anti-colonial struggle in the 1950s and the first euphoric years of independence in the 1960s. The 'Ibadan School', led from 1956 by Nigerian historian K. Onwuka Dike, came to be associated with a particular research agenda: a concern with the precolonial period, especially precolonial state formation; with the equation of 'trade and politics' in particular localities; with resistance to colonial conquest; and with the emergence in the 19th century of a literate African elite. Dike's *Trade and Politics in the Niger Delta* (1956) was the foundational text, a study of African-European interaction using European written sources but from a distinctly African perspective.

A determination to shatter the colonialist world view by linking the glories of the past to the dynamism of the present was shared by two scholars from outside the emerging system of university-trained professional historians, Basil Davidson and Thomas Hodgkin. Davidson, a campaigning journalist whose first of many books on African history and politics appeared in 1956, remains perhaps the single-most effective disseminator of the new field to a popular international audience. Hodgkin, who in the 1950s was an extra-mural teacher in the Gold Coast, captured the mood of the times in his influential *Nationalism in Colonial Africa* (1956), a work that set out to locate the emerging anti-colonial struggles in historical context. There has been much subsequent reflection on the part of historians on the ways that these agendas were shaped by the contemporary nation-building project. The search was on, in one evocative phrase, for a 'usable past' – a past where Africans had constructed viable states and which would be mobilized to show that they had survived the rupture of colonial conquest and were ready again to take control of their own destinies.

There is no doubt that the pioneering practitioners of African history, both African and European, professional and self-taught, felt a real sense of mission as the racial hierarchies of the imperial age crumbled about them. The notion of a 'usable' or 'legitimate' past, however, should not be exaggerated. Attention to the precolonial period on the part of early nationalist historians was determined as much by practical as by ideological reasons: in the 1950s and 1960s, the 50-year rule governing the release of official British documents (later reduced to 30 years) meant that the bulk of the colonial archive remained shut to researchers. With so much of the past a blank slate, moreover, it made sense to focus on what was most visible in the written and oral sources that were available that is, kingdoms and empires. These foundations were essential, it can be argued, for the later move to a broader social history.

More importantly, the past rarely presented political leaders with a readily usable model for the future. Whereas historians strove to bring to life in their writings powerful precolonial states, such as Asante, Buganda, and the Sokoto Caliphate, nationalist politicians sought not to resuscitate the political structures of the past but to inherit the territorial entities forged by European conquest. Nkrumah's struggle to integrate the Asante kingdom into the new nation state of Ghana and the equally uncomfortable incorporation of the Sokoto Caliphate into Nigeria and of Buganda into Uganda suggest the very real limits to the political function of historical knowledge. In short, African history as a political project was probably less important than the desire to establish its credentials as a legitimate part of the broader academic discipline.

Yet the epistemology of history as applied to Africa – that is, the theory of its grounds of knowledge – was contested from the outset. To continue with the example of Nigeria and the legacy of the Sokoto Caliphate, a rival school of historians based at Amadu Bello University in the northern city of Zaria emerged in the 1960s to challenge the intellectual hegemony of Ibadan. This group, who have been described as 'Islamic legitimists' and were led by a British convert to Islam, Abdullahi Smith, sought to find common ground between the methods of the new 'Western-style' African history and those of the older tradition of Muslim scholarship in the sudanic zone. By 1975, Smith was calling for a reorientation of Nigerian universities and of the discipline of history so that they might 'embody in their traditions something of the academic ideals of the Sokoto *jihad*'. As an early – albeit polite – challenge to the emerging dominance of 'Western' historical paradigms, his Northern History Research Scheme at Zaria was an indication of the ideological battles to come.

Abdullahi Smith's leading role in northern Nigeria exemplifies what would today be called the 'multicultural' nature of the anglophone historical project from the outset. This was the era when pioneering scholars such as Dike and Ajayi from Nigeria, A. Adu Boahen from Ghana, and Bethwell A. Ogot from Kenya, after completing their first degrees in the new African universities, continued their professional training by studying for PhDs in Britain before returning to build up history programmes in their home nations. This movement would come to include leading historians from Ethiopia and from South Africa – some of the latter, however, choosing not to return to the repressive environment of the apartheid state. It was also a time when European and North American scholars commonly spent extended periods teaching in

126

Africa. Many were attracted to the University of Dar es Salaam in Tanzania, which in the 1960s emerged as a centre of historical research to rival that at Ibadan. One was the radical Guyanese historian Walter Rodney, whose *How Europe Underdeveloped Africa* (1972) signalled a shift away from the 'nationalist' approach to more Marxist-influenced economic history.

Underpinning this intellectual exchange was the relative economic buoyancy of the developmental state, particularly during the commodity boom of the 1950s. In this respect, historians can be seen as part of the ranks of technical 'experts' who fanned out across the continent from the time of the postwar 'second colonial occupation' – this latter-day scramble being one for knowledge rather than territory. With the severe economic downturn of the 1970s, the brief expansionist phase in the continent's universities also came to an end. Budding African scholars continued to travel overseas to conduct doctoral training – increasingly to the United States – but more and more chose to remain abroad rather than return and face hardships at home.

The decolonization of history was slower to get going in French-ruled Africa. As in British colonies, the sheer pace of urbanization and social change forced French social scientists to re-evaluate received perceptions of static African 'tribes'. The most important work here was by Georges Balandier, who in 1951 published a perceptive essay on the changing 'colonial situation' and four years later a landmark study of African life in Brazzaville, the capital of French Equatorial Africa. Balandier would go on to play a leading role in the creation of new French Africanist institutions.

Unlike the anglophone world, however, history would remain a poor relation to anthropology in French scholarship for some time to come. A partial exception was the Maghrib, which benefited from a wealth of precolonial written sources in Arabic, an established tradition of Islamic scholarship, and, in Algeria, the existence of the colonial-era University of Algiers. In line with France's centralizing tradition, the only university in its tropical African empire at independence was at Dakar, in Senegal. But this was established in 1957 specifically as a French university on African soil, which, like the Sorbonne in Paris, continued to teach the history of colonization rather than that of African peoples. Even after independence in 1960, the University of Dakar remained fully integrated into the French system and the 'Africanization' of its teaching staff and its intellectual orientation was slow. As late as 1963, when there were still no Africans teaching history at Dakar, one of the first Senegalese students to have attained a doctorate in history, Abdoulaye Ly, commented that he would not apply to Paris for a job in his own country.

The importance of the professionalization of African history according to the recognized ground rules of the discipline should not obscure the fact that older 'vindicationist' traditions continued to evolve alongside – and in an uneasy dialogue with – university-based research. Partly because of the intellectual heritage of the *négritude* movement, but perhaps also because of the lingering colonialist outlook of the Sorbonne and the University of Dakar, these alternative, more speculative approaches to the African past were especially prominent in the francophone world. An important vehicle for the *négritude* tradition in its broadest sense was the journal *Présence Africaine*, founded in Paris in 1947 by the Senegalese intellectual Alioune Diop as a reaction against the ongoing assimilationist ideals of reformed French colonialism. It was *Présence Africaine* that in 1949 published Father Placide Tempels's *La philosophie bantou* ('Bantu Philosophy'), a universalist view of 'African thought' and the black creative spirit based on his missionary work in the Luba region of the Belgian Congo.

The towering figure in this milieu, however, was the Senegalese historical theorist Cheikh Anta Diop. Starting with his first book *Nations nègres et culture* (1955) – also published by *Présence Africaine* – Diop's work was fixated on the supposed cultural unity of pharaonic Egypt and sub-Saharan Africa. As noted in Chapter 2, this polemical theory has been convincingly rejected by archaeologists and historians on empirical grounds. Nonetheless, the dubious historical basis of Diop's speculations did not prevent his work from having a widespread impact – like the more sober contributions of Basil Davidson – far beyond the halls of academia. Importantly, Diop's outlook was also shaped by the anti-colonial struggle, and by the early 1960s he had entered Senegalese politics as a radical opposition voice to the government of poet-president Léopold Senghor. The continuing popular appeal of his Egypt-centric theories was underlined when a year after his death in 1986, the University of Dakar was renamed Cheikh Anta Diop University.

Postcolonial states

Unity *versus* diversity was not simply a scholarly debate about the nature of the African past. It was also a political issue that shaped the contours of the decolonization process and the ongoing conflicts of the postcolonial period. Elections in French and British Africa had served to focus political action on individual territories, where the real gains on offer diluted the old, vague ideals of pan-Africanist unity. In 1957, the Gold Coast became the first sub-Saharan African country to obtain full independence, the new nation adopting the name of the earliest of the great sudanic empires, Ghana. Guinea followed in 1958, its vote for full sovereignty rather than ongoing association with France precipitating the break-up and independence of the remainder of French Africa two years later. The year 1960 also saw the independence of Nigeria, Africa's most populous nation, Somalia, and the Belgian Congo.

This was a time of euphoria and huge optimism – indeed, a real moment of vindication. But despite the lofty rhetoric of Ghana's Kwame Nkrumah, the torch-bearer of pan-Africanism and advocate of 'continental government', it was becoming apparent that independence would be secured through the entrenchment of power in individual nation-states. With the sudden removal of the coercive underpinnings of European rule, moreover, the internal unity of a number of these new states was also thrown into doubt. Popular perceptions both inside and outside Africa often hold internal conflicts to be the result of reversion to some kind of primordial tribalism. As we have seen, however, recent research has demonstrated how ethnic identities and inter-regional rivalries were as often as not a product of colonial rule. Historians are only now becoming aware of just how complex the roots of social conflict and political violence in postcolonial Africa really are.

Nowhere was this tension between national unity and ethnic diversity more apparent than in the ex-Belgian Congo (now the Democratic Republic of Congo). Having tried and failed to insulate its huge central African domain against the winds of nationalism blowing through the rest of the continent, the highly authoritarian Belgian regime made a last-minute decision in the late 1950s to jump on the bandwagon of decolonization. The result was disaster. Within days of the hand-over of power in June 1960 to a government led by the charismatic nationalist Patrice Lumumba, the Congolese army had mutinied against the continuing control of its white officers. A week later, the mineral-rich southern region of Katanga seceded, plunging the Congo into years of recurring armed conflict that witnessed the murder of Lumumba by his enemies, the disintegration of the country into rival governments and ethnic fiefdoms, and foreign intervention.

Amidst fears of 'Soviet influence', on the one hand, and Western 'neocolonialism', on the other, the Congo became Africa's first Cold War battlefield. The so-called Congo Crisis (Congolese themselves referred to the period as the *pagaille*, 'the mess') was ended in 1965 with the recentralization of autocratic power following a military coup by ex-journalist turned general, Joseph Mobutu. Drawing on his own, warped vision of cultural and historical 'authenticity', Mobutu Sese Seko (as he became known after leading by example in the banning of 'colonialist' European names) became the ultimate in venal, corrupt African dictators, a new Leopold presiding over the latest incarnation of *bula matari*, the state as the 'breaker of rocks'.

The calamity of the Congo represents an extreme example of the failure of decolonization and of the postcolonial African state. The majority of the continent's new nations, in contrast, negotiated the transition to independence without experiencing such disastrous breakdown. Indeed, many enjoyed steady if unspectacular progress through the 1960s in the stated aim of their leaders: economic 'modernization' and 'national integration'. The momentum of anti-colonial nationalism was now unstoppable, carrying British East and Central Africa to independence in 1961–4, and igniting wars of liberation in the Portuguese colonies and, ultimately, against the breakaway white settler regime in Southern Rhodesia (Zimbabwe).

Despite continuing poverty and the general lack of democratic accountability, popular optimism generally remained high

26. African politics tangled with African American politics. Members of the Nation of Islam, holding placards with a portrait of murdered Congolese Prime Minister Patrice Lumumba, stage a counter-demonstration during a rally by the National Association for the Advancement of Colored People in Harlem, New York City, in 1961

throughout that decade. This was, to some extent, reflected in the first wave of African historiography. Even in the Congo, in the impoverished states of the sahelian zone, and in sprawling urban shanty towns stretching from the black 'townships' of apartheid South Africa north to Casablanca and Cairo, the resilience, innovation, and cultural vitality of the past continued. The quest for political freedom did not replace that for personal spiritual liberation, as the shift towards Islam and Christianity continued to accelerate in the second half of the 20th century. Most emblematically, new forms of popular music provided an infectious soundtrack to the struggles of day-to-day life and gave voice to aspirations for a better future. By the late 1960s, the most renowned *citoyen* of the Congo was not the political sorcerer Mobutu but guitar wizard Franco Luambo Makiadi, the leader of T.P.O.K. Jazz and Africa's first musical superstar. Franco's rumba sound swept the continent, transforming Mobutu's Congo (or Zaire, as the nation was renamed in 1971) from the heart of darkness of colonial and postcolonial mythmaking to the 'heart of danceness'. The recent expansion of historical research away from the political and economic and towards the social and cultural is beginning to reveal the dynamics of these underlying rhythms of everyday life.

By the late 1960s, however, the mood of optimism had turned distinctly sour. The widespread popular support in Ghana for the military *coup d'état* that in 1966 removed Kwame Nkrumah from power was an early indication that the promises of nationalist leaders were beginning to have a hollow ring. Yet one-party states gave way only to the 'no party states' of military dictatorships. A sequence of coups in the same year provided the catalyst for Nigeria's descent into civil war from 1967 to 1970. Nigeria emerged from the attempted Biafran secession intact, but under military rule and with the high hopes of independence all but extinguished.

Then, in the 1970s, came severe continent-wide economic downturn. The failure to diversify fragile economies away from a

27. **Popular culture. Dancers in Johannesburg in 1952, four years into the apartheid era. Photograph by Jürgen Schadeberg, one of the leading photographers on South Africa's famous *Drum* magazine**

dependence on the export of primary commodities meant that when the world economy went into recession following the oil crisis of 1973, the impact on Africa was devastating. In short, the end of the postwar boom spelt the end of the developmental state. Unable to provide the services now demanded by rapidly growing populations, the state itself began to contract, leaving increasing numbers of its citizens to fend for themselves as best they could. In the worst cases, it began to resemble its colonial predecessor: illegitimate, alien, and predatory. The deepening crisis also marked the end of the first phase of the new African history. As the high hopes of independence evaporated, a second generation of historians turned away from the achievements of indigenous state-builders and towards underlying economic and social struggles, struggles that often bridged the divide between precolonial and colonial (and by implication, at least, postcolonial) Africa.

Chapter 7
Memory and forgetting, past and present

Fifty years ago, in the mid-1950s, the notion of 'African history' barely existed. Beyond the speculative writings of a few African American intellectuals, the collections of oral traditions published by mission-educated Africans, and a handful of equally obscure translations of old Arabic chronicles, there was little or no scholarly engagement with the history of the continent. The study of Africa was dominated by the discipline of social anthropology, whose practitioners, if often highly sympathetic to African cultures, tended to portray them as timeless and unchanging. That part of the continent that did possess an established literate culture and therefore a recoverable past, the area to the north of the Sahara desert, was generally considered to belong more to the Mediterranean or the Arab world than to 'black Africa' to the south. Africa, in short, was deemed to be a realm apart, a continent without a history and whose future progress rested upon the continuation of European trusteeship.

Then came a revolution in thinking. As European colonialism crumbled, the recovery of the African past emerged as an integral part of the recovery of African sovereignty. From a tiny group of pioneers in the 1950s, the corps of Africanist historians expanded dramatically in subsequent decades, successfully forcing African history onto university curricula in Europe, in North America, and in Africa itself. In the face of a sceptical scholarly establishment and lacking much of the documentary evidence available to historians of other parts of the world, Africanists utilized a range of innovative sources and methods in order to give voice to peoples condemned by colonialism and by Eurocentrism to silence. In doing so, they achieved much: 'humanizing' Africa by reintegrating the continent into the broad sweep of history, while simultaneously enriching the academic discipline itself.

That, at least, is the received narrative. Like those African traditions of origin that memorialize founding fathers – the 'culture heroes' like Kalala Ilunga of the Luba who forged civilization on wild frontiers – it contains more than a kernel of truth. But like those traditions, too, the story is more complex and more contested. One thing, however, is clear: the optimistic, expansive phase of African history writing is now long gone. As early as the 1970s, a sense of uncertainty about the relevance and the direction of the academic enterprise was apparent. As Africa entered a period of prolonged economic downturn and political turmoil, the young field began to lurch from one dominant 'paradigm' to another. The postcolonial crisis also did lasting damage to the continent's universities: funding dried up, institutional and physical infrastructure crumbled, library collections deteriorated, and many historians opted to practise their craft overseas. Judging from the sense of anxiety that pervades recent historiographical surveys, African history seems to be in a state of ongoing crisis, divided over how best to maintain a dialogue between the past and the present, between the academic discipline and indigenous perceptions of the past, and, in the 'West', how best to engage with Africa-based scholars.

In this final chapter, we consider current developments in the study of African history. Where is the field heading? The changing ways of approaching the African past have, to some extent, continued to be fashioned by the shifting fortunes of the continent itself. At the start of the 21st century, only the most optimistic observer would suggest that either is in a state of rude health. Africa, especially sub-Saharan

Africa, is generally seen to be locked in permanent crisis. Widespread poverty, corruption, a lack of political accountability, ecological crises, famines, the HIV/AIDS pandemic, state collapse and civil war in places like Somalia, Sierra Leone, Liberia, Côte d'Ivoire, Darfur (in western Sudan), and the Democratic Republic of Congo: it appears sometimes that the *pagaille*, 'the mess' of the early years of Congolese independence, has engulfed the entire continent. This bleak landscape might suggest that Africa is still viewed by jaundiced outsiders as somehow 'pathological', as disordered and abnormal. But this is also a view widely held by a great many ordinary Africans themselves. How should the study of the past speak to this troubled present?

Memory and forgetting

First, two stories about memory, forgetting, and history in modern Africa. For the first, we return to the Republic of Mali, where we began the book with an account of Jenne-jeno. Its central character is Waa Kamisòkò (c. 1919–1976), a famous *jeli* (oral traditionist or 'griot') of the Manden, the Mande heartland of the old Mali empire on the upper reaches of the Niger River. Waa Kamisòkò's career, as examined by P. F. de Moraes Farias, tells us much about the tension between the past and the present in the preservation of memory and the reproduction of history. Like other *jeliw*, he specialized in performing the cycle of songs and narratives comprising the epic of Sunjata, the 13th-century founder of Mali, as well as those concerning its greatest ruler, Mansa Musa, who famously performed the pilgrimage to Mecca in 1324–5. More unusually, he also developed a close relationship with academic scholarship, participating in international historical seminars and collaborating with the Malian anthropologist Y. T. Cissé in the translation (into French) and publication of his version of the Sunjata epic.

Perhaps because of these links with academics, but perhaps too because of his broader personal experience of modern Mali, Waa Kamisòkò moved beyond the conventional role of *jeli* and of historical 'informant'. He did so by insinuating his own critical commentary into established narratives. As we noted in Chapter 3, oral traditions are often reshaped by the political milieu in which they are recounted. They tend to legitimate the status quo – to the extent that in modern Mali, *jeliw* have been recruited by the ruling elite in order to justify political authoritarianism. Waa Kamisòkò, however, was often critical of revered historical figures and of Mali's nationalist leadership in the 1960s–70s. In his interpretation of the Sunjata epic and his narratives of the history of enslavement, for example, he made a case for the greater acknowledgement of the contribution of marginalized caste groups (*nyamankala*) and of people of slave ancestry to past as well as present Mandenka society.

It was Waa Kamisòkò's views on Islam that proved most controversial. Like many Malians, his personal religious identity was complex, encompassing both Islam and indigenous religion. A member of the cult association of Kirina Kònò, the 'Bird of Krina', centred on his native village of Krina, he was often critical of what he saw as the destructive impact of Islam on older Mandenka culture. At a time of rising debate between 'neo-traditionalists', who viewed Islam as essentially alien to African culture, and purist Muslim reformists, who regarded pagan cults such as Kirina Kònò with disdain, Waa Kamisòkò used his oral performances to emphasize the history of co-existence between the two belief systems. He drew parallels between Mansa Musa's 'excessive' devotion to Islam and the militancy of contemporary reformists, while reflecting upon the ways in which Islamic motifs had overlaid older accounts of Mandenka history. His interpretation of the past, like that of the archaeologists working at Jenne-jeno, represented a critique of the established narrative of the 'imperial tradition'.

For our second story, we move to Zimbabwe, to the Nkayi and Lupane districts of northern Matabeleland. In contrast to the Manden, a long-settled heartland with a high degree of cultural continuity, this is a frontier region with a tumultuous recent past. It is also characterized by the absence of local historical texts or of 'organic intellectuals' such as Waa Kamisòkò. Much of the past appears to be forgotten. Nkayi and Lupane were encompassed in the colonial period by the Shangani Reserve, one of two 'native reserves' set aside for the settlement of the Ndebele people during the British occupation of what was then Southern Rhodesia in the 1890s. Displaced Ndebele chiefs and their followers began to move into the Shangani forests in the 1910s, settling amongst scattered populations speaking Tonga, Shangwe, and other languages and, to some extent, adapting to local cultures. The influx increased after the Second World War. By then, according to Terence Ranger, many Ndebele were self-consciously modern, progressive Christians. They retained their Ndebele identity, often lumping the original peoples of the Shangani together as 'Zambezis'. The latter in turn referred to them as *daluka*, 'the dumped ones'. 'It was difficult, if not impossible', Ranger argues, 'to evolve a common local history'.

This does not mean that the diverse peoples of the Shangani have no sense of the past. 'History', however, is recent history. Ranger and his research collaborators have identified two grand narratives, both of which deal with the period after the Second World War. One is that of the Ndebele evictees, a saga of an uprooted people bringing civilized values to a frontier wilderness. The other is that of nationalism, which came to a climax in the guerrilla war against the white minority regime in the 1970s and the post-independence struggles against Robert Mugabe's ZANU (Zimbabwe African National Union) government in the 1980s. As in many other parts of Africa, the narrative of nationalist struggle overlays older, local mosaics of memory, sometimes silencing and at other times amplifying them.

This process of engagement between different layers of the past emerges in Ranger's account of a ceremony of remembrance planned in 1992 for those ZAPU (Zimbabwe African People's Union) fighters killed in the guerrilla war. The site chosen was Pupu, in the Lupane district, the location of the Ndebele king Lobengula's last battle as well as that of the 'last stand' of a British

South Africa Company patrol in 1893. During the bush war in the 1960s–70s, ZAPU guerrillas had visited the old battlefield in order to draw strength from the Ndebele military tradition. The projected ceremony, however, was controversial. The Mugabe government was suspicious, fearing a revival of Ndebele kingship or of local loyalty to ZAPU. The population of Pupu, moreover, was diverse, and many non-Ndebele were unhappy about linking the nationalist struggle so explicitly to Lobengula and his famous father, Mzilikazi. Indeed, as the different participants gathered on the night before 'Heroes Day', a medium was possessed by the spirit of a Rozwi *mambo*, one of the local rulers who had been superseded by the Ndebele. 'The medium demanded recognition for this older past and the healing of its violences', Ranger writes. 'A history rarely articulated was breaking through in ritual.'

28. **Postcolonial violence. A soldier of the National Union for the Total Independence of Angola (UNITA) poses next to an upturned colonial statue in Nova Lisboa (now Huambo) on 12 November 1975, following the collapse of Portuguese rule. Nearly two decades of civil war between UNITA and the rival MPLA government was to follow**

Remembering the present

These two cases illustrate a number of themes that in recent years have begun to emerge in the study of African history. One is a concern with intellectual history; that is, the ways and means by which people have thought about things and have represented them. As we saw in Chapter 1 with the rise of environmental history, new research agendas are often part of broader shifts in the discipline or in academic fashion more generally. But they are also shaped by the particularities of the African past – and the African present. Both studies are histories about history. As such, they are reflective of wider concerns about intellectual production and contested representations: the so-called 'cultural-linguistic turn' in the humanities loosely associated with the idea of postmodernism. Yet they also have a specifically African context: the imperative amongst historians of the continent to interrogate the relationship between past and present, as well as that between indigenous perceptions of history, on the one hand, and their own craft, on the other.

The influence of the present over perceptions of the past has been evident throughout the evolution of the new African history. The first major reorientation in the field was a shift in the 1970s beyond the initial focus on state-building towards what can be described as political economy. This involved, in some cases, a more ideologically radical agenda, notably the 'dependency theory' approach exemplified by Walter Rodney's *How Europe Underdeveloped Africa* (1972) and research by French Marxist anthropologists into the configuration of economic systems (labelled 'modes of production'). As these varieties of Marxist analysis represented an attempt to apply more universal categories to Africa, it is interesting to note just how limited their influence was. By the mid-1980s, they were already fading from view, suggesting that Western social science theory did indeed sit uncomfortably with African realities. But Marxist anthropology did have a lasting legacy. By emphasizing the differentials in economic and social power between rich and poor, young and old, men and women, free and unfree, it made a crucial contribution to the breaking down of lingering perceptions of homogenous states, tribes, and kinship groups. This invigorated research into several key areas: slavery, gender, and, because of its concern with the workings of capitalism, the one region where Marxist analysis had particular purchase: modern South Africa.

In a continent with very limited industrialization or class formation, Marxist economic analysis could only go so far. But its emphasis on social struggles opened the way for the development of a broader-based social history, a history not of high politics and 'great men', but of ordinary men and women. As Africa's political leadership revealed itself to be anything but great, more historians concerned themselves with exploring the underlying rhythms of everyday life. For this, of course, they needed evidence: the written records and oral testimonies that reveal the actions, motivations, beliefs, and aspirations of common people. Here, in part, lies the reason for the growing volume of research on the 20th century. It is not that a deeper, more 'authentic' African past has been abandoned by historians now only interested in colonialism. It is more that the desire to reconstruct an Africa populated by individual actors in all their complexity and idiosyncrasy rather than by faceless collectivities ('tribes') has drawn historians inexorably towards recent times.

That said, historians of Africa, like all historians, must be careful not to impose their own ways of seeing the world on different cultures and on past times. This is as true for those who are African themselves as for non-Africans; as Paulo Farias has noted with regard to medieval inscriptions in eastern Mali, they were produced in an intellectual universe far removed even from those who now live in the same place. It also holds for the more recent past. Many African societies did have a powerful collective ethos into which individual aspiration and autonomous action were submerged – even if this ethos was not quite as communal as once thought. 'The anonymity of individuals in much of the evidence', Joseph Miller writes, 'thus becomes less a deficiency of the sources than a window opening onto Africans' collective ways of thinking'.

Such collective thought emerges in the notion of 'witchcraft', a concept that in many African societies explains both misfortune *and* excessive individual fortune. That witchcraft is now attracting the interest of historians is due in part to its continuing prominence, including in the political realm. The language of witchcraft, in short, has been used to explain the 'vampiric' power of the colonial and postcolonial state, just as in earlier times it seems to have been used to comprehend the malevolence of the slave trade. All these alien forces consume wealth or consume people, just as witches were seen to 'eat' the souls of their victims. It is this perception of consumption – sometimes played upon to full effect by figures such as Mobutu Sese Seko – that political scientist Jean-François Bayart has called 'the politics of the belly'.

Witchcraft narratives, then, like those of early modern Europe, are not simply stories of the freakish or the occult. They are key components of a broader intellectual and cultural history of Africa. Arising from this intellectual history is a more specific concern with the idea of memory. From the very outset, historians sought to tap into the stores of indigenous memory passed orally from generation to generation. As the analytical challenges of oral tradition became apparent, so too did the sheer diversity of genres representing 'history' in African societies. Historical memory, rather than simply being recounted as a set of codified events, is often 'performed' – as epic narrative, as ritual, as praise poetry, as visual art, or even during a tape-recorded interview with a researcher. Far from transferring immutable, collective traditions, such genres allow for personalized reflection and reinterpretation. They are also in many cases entangled with written history, both that produced by academics and by local intellectuals. This is evident in the case of Waa Kamisòkò, whose dialogue with academics influenced his interpretations of tradition. It emerges too in the evocative historical paintings produced since the 1970s by Congolese artists such as Tshibumba Kanda-Matulu, some of which were commissioned by Western scholars. In the words of one of those scholars, the anthropologist Johannes Fabian, Kanda-Matulu and other painters were engaged in the task of 'remembering the present'.

Yet memory, like all visions of the past, is selective. Some things are recalled, but many others are forgotten. And while popular memory

29. Samuel Fosso, *Le chef: celui qui a vendu l'Afrique aux colons*, from the series Série Tati, autoportraits I–V, 1997. 'The chief who sold Africa to the colonists.' One of contemporary Africa's most famous artists, Fosso, based in Bangui in the Central African Republic, masquerades in this 'autoportrait' as the self-styled omnipotent ruler, a subversive portrayal of the image of Congolese dictator Mobutu Sese Seko and the regalia of indigenous kingship

may hold one version of events to be true, 'official memory' may be something quite different. This is as true for Africa today as it was in the past, when those who came out on top in political struggles got to tell the stories sanctified as tradition. In forging their own historical vision, Waa Kamisòkò in Mali and Tshibumba Kanda-Matulu in Congo/Zaire both tapped into streams of popular memory often running counter to received versions of the past. They can be seen, to some extent, to be 'counter-hegemonic'. Elsewhere, such as in the northern Matabeleland region of Zimbabwe, alternative historical memories are more deeply submerged by dominant narratives. And, as the case of Matabeleland indicates, the one narrative that has most often been laid across older, deeper currents is that of nationalism.

This brings us to a final development in African history writing: a growing interest in the continent's 'contemporary' history. What exactly constitutes the contemporary is unclear, but in the African context the term seems to be broadly synonymous with the postcolonial era. Just as historians came gradually to engage with the complexities of colonialism, so the research frontier is now moving into the second half of the 20th century. We touched on some emerging themes in the last chapter, especially the patterns of continuity and change that characterized the shift from colonial empires to nation-states. What is starting to become clear is that this political transition is just one of many histories, which have often been drowned out by the narrative of anti-colonial liberation and the forging of new states. Many who fought for freedom from colonial oppression found their stories silenced by political rivals, who once in power strove to forget the struggles of past in the pursuit of 'national unity'. The ZAPU militants in Matabeleland are just one example. Another is that of the forest fighters of the Mau Mau rebellion in 1950s Kenya, a conflict that was at once an anti-colonial uprising and a civil war within Kikuyu society. As Ranger suggests, the recognition of all these stories will be necessary to heal the violence of the past and the tensions of the present.

African history, African heritage

The year 2007 marks the 200th anniversary of the Abolition of the Slave Trade Act. After a long campaign by abolitionists, the British parliament finally voted to outlaw the transportation of slaves in British ships, effective from 1 May 1807. It was not the first such legislation: some individual states of the United States had already prohibited the trade, as had Denmark. Revolutionary France, meanwhile, in the aftermath of the huge slave uprising in its Caribbean colony of Saint Domingue (Haiti) in 1791, had declared an end to the slave trade and to the institution of slavery, only for both to be reinstated by Napoleon in 1802. Nor was abolition immediately effective. Africans continued to be exported across the Atlantic in large numbers until mid-century, while slavery itself continued in Brazil and Cuba until the 1880s and in many parts of Africa well into the 20th century. Yet for all its ambiguity, 1807 represents a key moment in the making of the modern world. Its bicentenary should stimulate reflection on the relationship between African history and the broader human history of which it is part.

Slavery also brings us back to where we began: to the invention of Africa. The idea of Africa, it will be remembered, emerged in part from the experience of the transatlantic slave trade. Is there, then, such a thing as African history, or is there just history, as it happened to unfold on the continent called Africa? In the end, any answer to this question will be subjective. All assertions about the past of anywhere are at once assertions about the particular and assertions about the universality of knowledge and historical 'truth'. Yet many would argue that if there is a distinctively African past, then it is one forged, at least over the past few centuries, by a sequence of traumatic historical experiences: the slave trades; the tumult of the 19th century; colonial conquest; and the ongoing poverty, violence, and political authoritarianism of the era of independence. None of these episodes can be characterized simply as unmitigated disasters for all Africans; as we have seen, their effects have been far more complex and differentiated than often recognized. African societies survived the challenges of the past, and will survive those of the present. Yet the impact of this succession of traumas on the lived experience of Africans and on the formulation of the idea of Africa itself must not be underestimated. The question is how best to recover and to represent this history of suffering, of struggle, and of resilience.

Emerging in the heady years of anti-colonial struggle and national liberation, African history as an academic endeavour from the outset had a mission. It set out to rectify past wrongs; to change the world – or at least how its past was envisaged. For some historians, this has been its strength; for others, its weakness. All would probably agree that the responsibility to transform the established idea of history as well as to help transform Africa itself was a heavy burden to carry. Divisions were bound to arise; and they soon did: over questions of race and power within universities and professional associations, over the relevance of Western historical epistemologies to the African past, over the degree to which history writing should be an academic exercise or a political project. These debates played out mainly in the United States – not just because of the intensity of its own racial politics, but because it soon surpassed the old colonial powers and independent Africa itself as the principal centre of African historical research. As early as 1969, some black members of the US African Studies Association split from the main body to pursue a more pan-Africanist agenda in the rival African *Heritage* Studies Association. The racial divide was never absolute, and these days ASA meetings are attended by black and white scholars from the US, Africa, and beyond. But debates over the relationship between history and heritage – the latter implying something that is inherited, and therefore 'owned' – continue to arise.

Such 'heritage wars' are not peculiar to the African past. They have been especially prominent in India in recent years, fuelled by the rise of militant Hindu nationalism. They also characterize recent debates over how British history should be taught in schools: a grand narrative of national glories, or a grittier, more inclusive 'history from below' that for some makes unpleasant reading. The memorialization of the slave trade is one area where this question looms large. And it cuts both ways: a version of the slave trade that fails to come to grips with the active participation of African ruling elites is as partial and as sanitized as a version of British history in which its own participation in the trade is downplayed.

Another is the history of South Africa. The final collapse of the apartheid regime and the coming to power of Nelson Mandela and the African National Congress is a key event in recent world history. The ANC's 1994 election victory, just weeks after the horrors of the Rwandan genocide, represented a beacon of hope for the future. It can be seen as the final act in the long process of African decolonization (leaving aside, that is, the ongoing Moroccan occupation of the Western Sahara), and came at a time of mounting popular pressure across much of the continent for an end to autocratic rule and for free, multi-party elections. The political struggle for the present is, for the moment, resolved; what remains is representing and reconciling the struggles of the past.

One of the many tasks that now faces a democratic South Africa is how to rethink and to rewrite its history. How should history be taught in schools and universities? Should the process inaugurated by the county's Truth and Reconciliation Commission be about forgiving and forgetting, or about righting past wrongs? In the dark years of the apartheid regime, the past had been hijacked by those with power. History was dominated by the grand narrative of white settlement; by the battles fought by the emerging Afrikaner nation against the 'Bantu' and the British empire to hold and to civilize the land. But the counter-narrative, that of a triumphant black African nationalism, is equally simplistic. It too silences as much as it reveals: a glossed-over heritage rather than history. In the words of Shula Marks, one of the leading historians of South Africa, the challenge lies in transforming the nation's past from a simple 'morality play' to a history in all its complexity and ambiguity.

Is African history still relevant, as it so clearly was in the era of national liberation? The answer must be a resounding 'yes'. Africa's contemporary crisis often makes the task of researching, writing, and teaching its history a huge challenge – especially for those scholars who labour under difficult circumstances in the continent's struggling universities. Yet we would argue that just as the triumphant claims of the 'nationalist' phase of history writing were somewhat exaggerated, so too are current anxieties about the state of the field. This is not to downplay the difficulties ahead. It is to suggest, however, that the severity of Africa's crisis makes an understanding of how it got to be where it is today as important as it ever was.

References

Chapter 1

Edward Said, *Orientalism: Western Conceptions of the Orient* (New York, 1978).

John Iliffe, *Africans: The History of a Continent* (Cambridge, 1995), p. 1.

Frederick Cooper, *Africa since 1940: The Past of the Present* (Cambridge, 2002).

James C. McCann, *Green Land, Brown Land, Black Land: An Environmental History of Africa, 1800–1990* (Portsmouth, NH, 1999), p. 3.

Roderick J. McIntosh, *The Peoples of the Middle Niger: The Island of Gold* (Oxford, 1998), p. xv.

Chapter 2

T. E. Bowdich, *Mission from Cape Coast Castle to Ashantee* (London, 1967 [1819]), p. 43.

W. E. Burghardt Du Bois, *The Negro* (New York, 1915).

Martin Bernal, *Black Athena: The Afroasiatic Roots of Classical Civilization* (London, 1987).

Samuel Johnson, *The History of the Yorubas* (Lagos, 1921).

Lee Cronk, *From Mokogodo to Maasai: Ethnicity and Cultural Change in Kenya* (Boulder, 2004).

Chapter 3

Jan Vansina, *Art History in Africa: An Introduction to Method* (London, 1984), p. 135.

Paul Jenkins (ed.), *The Recovery of the West African Past: African Pastors and African History in the Nineteenth Century* (Basel, 1998).

Jan Vansina, *Oral History: A Study in Historical Methodology* (Chicago, 1965).

Joseph C. Miller, 'History and Africa/Africa and History', *American Historical Review*, 104 (1999), p. 11.

Thomas Q. Reefe, *The Rainbow and the Kings: A History of the Luba Empire to 1891* (Berkeley, 1981).

John Yoder, *The Kanyok of Zaire: An Institutional and Ideological History to 1895* (Cambridge, 1992).

Susan Keech McIntosh, 'Archaeology and the Reconstruction of the African Past', in John Edward Philips (ed.), *Writing African History* (Rochester, 2005), p. 57.

Henry John Drewal, 'Signs of Time, Shapes of Thought: The Contribution of Art History and Visual Culture to Historical Methods in Africa', in Philips, *Writing African History*, pp. 330 and 332.

Chapter 4

Jean-François Bayart, 'Africa in the World: A History of Extraversion', *African Affairs*, 99 (2000), p. 218.

C. A. Bayly, *The Birth of the Modern World 1780-1914: Global Connections and Comparisons* (Oxford, 2004).

John Thornton, *The Kongolese Saint Anthony: Dona Beatriz Kimpa Vita and the Antonian Movement, 1684-1706* (Cambridge, 1998).

J. D. Y. Peel, *Religious Encounter and the Making of the Yoruba* (Bloomington, 2000).

Jean Comaroff and John Comaroff, *Of Revelation and Revolution: Christianity, Colonialism and Consciousness in South Africa* (Chicago, 1991).

John Thornton, *Africa and Africans in the Making of the Atlantic World, 1400-1800* (Cambridge, 1998).

Robin Law and Paul E. Lovejoy (eds), *The Biography of Mahommah Gardo Baquaqua: His Passage From Slavery to Freedom in Africa and America* (Princeton, 2001).

Patrick Manning, 'Africa and the African Diaspora: New Directions of Study', *Journal of African History*, 44 (2003), p. 490.

Chapter 5

Jacob F. Ade Ajayi, 'Colonialism: An Episode in African History', in L. Gann and P. Duignan (eds), *Colonialism in Africa* Vol. 1 (Cambridge, 1969).

Frederick Cooper, *Colonialism in Question: Theory, Knowledge, History* (Berkelcy, 2005), p. 34.

Jan Vansina, *Paths in the Rainforest: Towards a History of Political Tradition in Equatorial Africa* (Madison, 1990).

David Robinson, *Paths of Accommodation: Muslim Societies and French Colonial Authorities in Senegal and Mauritania, 1880–1920* (Athens, Ohio, 2000).

Sir Apolo Kaggwa, *Kings of Buganda*, tr. M. Kiwanuka (Nairobi, 1971).

David Cannadine, *Ornamentalism: How the British Saw Their Empire* (London, 2001).

Niall Ferguson, *Empire: The Rise and Demise of the British World Order and the Lessons for Global Power* (London, 2002).

Jomo Kenyatta, *Facing Mount Kenya: The Tribal Life of the Gikuyu* (London, 1938).

Terence Ranger, 'The Invention of Tradition in Colonial Africa', in E. J. Hobsbawm and T. O. Ranger (eds), *The Invention of Tradition* (Cambridge, 1983).

Mahmood Mamdani, *Citizen and Subject: Contemporary Africa and the Legacy of Late Colonialism* (Princeton, 1996).

Chapter 6

Jacob F. Ade Ajayi, 'African History at Ibadan', in A. H. M. Kirk-Greene (ed.), *The Emergence of African History at British Universities* (Oxford, 1995), p. 93.

K. O. Dike, *Trade and Politics in the Niger Delta, 1830–1885* (London, 1956).

Thomas Hodgkin, *Nationalism in Colonial Africa* (London, 1956).

Paul E. Lovejoy, 'Nigeria: The Ibadan School and its Critics', in Bogumil Jewsiewicki and David Newbury (eds), *African Historiographies: What History for Which Africa?* (Beverly Hills, 1986), p. 202.

Walter Rodney, *How Europe Underdeveloped Africa* (London, 1972).

Martin A. Klein, 'The Development of Senegalese Historiography', in Jewsiewicki and Newbury, *African Historiographies*, p. 217.

Chapter 7

P. F. de Moraes Farias, 'The Oral Traditionist as Critic and Intellectual Producer: An Example from Contemporary Mali', in Toyin Falola (ed.), *African Historiography: Essays in Honour of Jacob Ade Ajayi* (Harlow, 1993).

Terence Ranger, 'African Local Historiographies: A Negative Case', in Axel Harneit-Sievers (ed.), *A Place in the World: New Local Historiographies from Africa and South Asia* (Leiden, 2002), pp. 293 and 302.

Joseph C. Miller, 'History and Africa/Africa and History', *American Historical Review*, 104 (1999), p. 21.

Jean-François Bayart, *The State in Africa: The Politics of the Belly* (Harlow, 1993).

Johannes Fabian, *Remembering the Present: Painting and Popular History in Zaire* (Berkeley, 1996).

Shula Marks, 'Rewriting South African History', in Simon McGrath *et al.* (eds), *Rethinking African History* (Edinburgh, 1997).

Further reading

Chapter 1

Philosophers rather than historians have pioneered scholarship on the idea of Africa: see V. Y. Mudimbe, *The Invention of Africa: Gnosis, Philosophy, and the Order of Knowledge* (Bloomington, 1988), and *The Idea of Africa* (Bloomington, 1994), and Kwame Anthony Appiah, *In My Father's House: Africa and the Philosophy of Culture* (New York, 1992). For comparative insights, see Ronald B. Inden, *Imagining India* (Oxford, 1990), and Chris Wickham, *Framing the Early Middle Ages: Europe and the Mediterranean, 400–800* (Oxford, 2005). From a geographical perspective, Martin W. Lewis and Kären E. Wigen, *The Myth of Continents: A Critique of Metageography* (Berkeley, 1997) is thought-provoking. The best one-volume survey of African history is John Iliffe, *Africans: The History of a Continent* (Cambridge, 1995). James C. McCann, *Green Land, Brown Land, Black Land: An Environmental History of Africa, 1800–1990* (Portsmouth, NH, 1999) is an excellent introduction. Roderick J. McIntosh, *The Peoples of the Middle Niger: The Island of Gold* (Oxford, 1998) is a superb work of historical archaeology. For the broader context, see Graham Connah, *African Civilizations. Precolonial Cities and States: An Archaeological Perspective* (2nd edn, Cambridge, 2001), David W. Phillipson, *African Archaeology* (3rd edn, Cambridge, 2005), and David M. Anderson and Richard Rathbone (eds), *Africa's Urban Past* (Oxford, 2000). On Sunjata, see Ralph Austen (ed.), *In Search of Sunjata: The Mande Epic as History, Literature, and Performance* (Bloomington, 1999).

Chapter 2

For an introduction to the history of Africa's populations, see James L. Newman, *The Peopling of Africa: A Geographic Interpretation* (New Haven, 1995), and for its languages, B. Heine and D. Nurse (eds), *African Languages: An Introduction* (Cambridge, 2000). On North Africa, Michael Brett and Elizabeth Fentress, *The Berbers* (Oxford, 1996) is excellent. For hybrid coastal communities, try John Middleton, *The World of the Swahili: An African Mercantile Civilization* (New Haven, 1992), and George Brooks, *Eurafricans in Western Africa* (Athens, Ohio, 2003). For a robust critique of Afrocentrism, see Stephen Howe, *Afrocentrism: Mythical Pasts and Imagined Homes* (London, 1998). On identity and historical imagination in South Africa, see Carolyn Hamilton, *Terrific Majesty: The Powers of Shaka Zulu and the Limits of Historical Invention* (Cambridge, Mass., 1998), and T. Dunbar Moodie, *The Rise of Afrikanerdom: Power, Apartheid and Afrikaner Civil Religion* (Berkeley, 1975), and on the Yoruba, Toyin Falola (ed.), *Yoruba Historiography* (Madison, 1991), and L. J. Matory, 'The English Professors of Brazil: On the Diasporic Roots of the Yoruba Nation', *Comparative Studies in Society and History*, 41 (1999). For precolonial Rwanda, see Jan Vansina, *Antecedents to Modern Rwanda: The Nyiginya Kingdom* (Oxford, 2004), and for the 20th century, Mahmood Mamdani, *When Victims Become Killers: Colonialism, Nativism, and the Genocide in Rwanda* (Princeton, 2001). A history of popular music in Africa remains to be written, but for a regional study, try G. Stewart, *Rumba on the River: A History of the Popular Music of the Two Congos* (London, 2000).

Chapter 3

For useful introductions to the issues of evidence and method in African history, see the essays in John Edward Philips (ed.), *Writing African History* (Rochester, 2005); ongoing developments are examined in the journal *History in Africa*. Tadesse Tamrat, *Church and State in Ethiopia, 1270–1527* (Oxford, 1972) is a classic account of medieval Ethiopia using the region's rich documentary sources. Amongst critical editions of Arabic sources for sub-Saharan history, N. Levtzion and J. F. P. Hopkins (eds), *Corpus of Early Arabic Sources for West African*

History (Cambridge, 1981), and John O. Hunwick, *Timbuktu and the Songhay Empire: Al-Sa'dî's Ta'rîkh al-Sûdân down to 1613* (Leiden, 1999) are outstanding; so too is Paulo F. de Moraes Farias, *Arabic Medieval Inscriptions from the Republic of Mali: Epigraphy, Chronicles, and Songhay-Tuâreg History* (Oxford, 2003). On oral narratives, try Isabel Hofmeyr, *'We Spend Our Years as a Tale That is Told': Oral Historical Narrative in a South African Chiefdom* (Portsmouth, NH, 1994). Sally Falk Moore, *Anthropology and Africa: Changing Perspectives on a Changing Scene* (Charlottesville, 1994) is a useful guide. For two examples of the possibilities of art history, see Paula Girshick Ben-Amos, *Art, Innovation, and Politics in Eighteenth-Century Benin* (Bloomington, 1999), and Mary Nooter Roberts and Allen F. Roberts (eds), *Memory: Luba Art and the Making of History* (New York, 1996). On photographs as historical sources, including commentary on some of the images used in this book, see *African Arts*, Special Issue: Historical Photographs of Africa, 24, 4 (1991), and on literature, Margaret Jean Hay (ed.), *African Novels in the Classroom* (Boulder, 2000).

Chapter 4

On locating Africa in world history, see Steven Feierman, 'African Histories and the Dissolution of World History', in Robert H. Bates, V. Y. Mudimbe, and Jean O'Barr (eds), *Africa and the Disciplines* (Chicago, 1993). On Kongo religious history, see Wyatt MacGaffey, *Modern Kongo Prophets* (Bloomington, 1983), and for the broader context, Adrian Hastings, *The Church in Africa, 1450–1950* (Oxford, 1994). The best introduction to Islam is David Robinson's *Muslim Societies in African History* (Cambridge, 2004); see too Nehemia Levtzion and Randal Pouwels (eds), *The History of Islam in Africa* (Athens, Ohio, 2000). From a huge literature on slavery and the slave trade, see Joseph C. Miller, *Way of Death: Merchant Capitalism and the Angolan Slave Trade, 1730–1830* (Madison, 1988), Paul E. Lovejoy, *Transformations in Slavery: A History of Slavery in Africa* (2nd edn, Cambridge, 2000), and Boubacar Barry, *Senegambia and the Atlantic Slave Trade* (Cambridge, 1998). David Eltis, Stephen D. Behrendt, David Richardson, and Herbert S. Klein, *The Trans-Atlantic Slave*

Trade: A Database on CD-ROM (Cambridge, 1999) is an extraordinary achievement. For the Nigerian Hinterland Project, go to *www.yorku.ca/ nhp*. Michael A. Gomez, *Reversing Sail: A History of the African Diaspora* (Cambridge, 2005) is a good introduction. Much recent research can be found in the journal *Slavery and Abolition*: see especially Vol. 22, 1 (2001), special issue on 'Rethinking the African Diaspora' edited by Kristin Mann and Edna G. Bay. On Madagascar, see Pier M. Larson, *History and Memory in the Age of Enslavement: Becoming Merina in Highland Madagascar 1770–1822* (Portsmouth, NH, 2000).

Chapter 5

The best account of conquest from the African perspective is John Lonsdale, 'The European Scramble and Conquest in African History', in *Cambridge History of Africa* Vol. 6 (Cambridge, 1985); for a more conventional narrative, see Thomas Pakenham, *The Scramble for Africa* (London, 1991). Jonathan Glassman, *Feasts and Riot: Revelry, Rebellion and Popular Consciousness on the Swahili Coast, 1856–1888* (Portsmouth, NH, 1995) examines the local underbelly of the German conquest of the coast of Tanzania. On the impact of colonial rule, John Iliffe, *A Modern History of Tanganyika* (Cambridge, 1979) is a classic; for women's experiences, begin with Jean Allman, Susan Geiger, and Nakanyike Musisi (eds), *Women in Colonial African Histories* (Bloomington, 2002). For a lively account of how one village community negotiated the 20th century, see Landeg White, *Magomero: Portrait of an African Village* (Cambridge, 1987); and for another, which straddles the coming of colonial rule, T. C. McCaskie, *Asante Identities: History and Modernity in an African Village, 1850–1950* (Edinburgh, 2000). On the circulation of ideas, see Andrew Roberts (ed.), *The Colonial Moment in Africa: Essays on the Movement of Minds and Materials, 1900–1940* (Cambridge, 1990). On the invention of tradition and indirect rule, see T. O. Ranger, 'The Invention of Tradition Revisited', in T.O. Ranger and Olafemi Vaughan (eds), *Legitimacy and the State in Twentieth-Century Africa* (London, 1993), and Thomas Spear, 'Neo-Traditionalism and the Limits of Invention in British Colonial Africa', *Journal of African History*, 44 (2003).

Chapter 6

On the impact of the war on Africa, see David Killingray and Richard Rathbone (eds), *Africa and the Second World War* (London, 1986). The postwar moment has been analysed with insight by Frederick Cooper in his *Africa since 1940: The Past of the Present* (Cambridge, 2002). J. D. Hargreaves, *Decolonization in Africa* (2nd edn, London, 1996) is a useful survey. The literature on the decolonization of Ghana is particularly well developed: see Jean Allman, *The Quills of the Porcupine: Asante Nationalism in an Emergent Ghana* (Madison, 1993), and Richard Rathbone, *Nkrumah and the Chiefs: The Politics of Chieftaincy in Ghana, 1951–1960* (Oxford, 1999); so too is that on the Mau Mau rebellion: John Lonsdale, 'The Moral Economy of Mau Mau', in Bruce Berman and John Lonsdale, *Unhappy Valley: Conflict in Kenya and Africa* Vol. 2 (London, 1992), and David Anderson, *Histories of the Hanged: Britain's Dirty War in Kenya and the End of Empire* (London, 2005). Alistair Horne, *A Savage War of Peace: Algeria, 1954–1962* (London, 1977) is a classic. The British Documents on the End of Empire project is a key resource: the latest in the series is Philip Murphy, *Central Africa*, two volumes (London, 2005). On the emergence of African history, a good place to start is the lively memoir of one of the pioneers, Jan Vansina, *Living with Africa* (Madison, 1994), and for the pan-Africanist tradition, V. Y. Mudimbe (ed.), *The Surreptitious Speech: Présence Africaine and the Politics of Otherness, 1947–1987* (Chicago, 1992). For a typically trenchant commentary on *négritude* and on Africa's postcolonial predicament, see Wole Soyinka, *The Burden of Memory, the Muse of Forgiveness* (New York, 1999).

Chapter 7

Stephen Ellis, 'Writing Histories of Contemporary Africa', *Journal of African History*, 43 (2002), surveys the challenges of recent history. On memory, see Jocelyn Alexander, JoAnn McGregor, and Terence Ranger, *Violence and Memory: One Hundred Years in the Dark Forests of Matabeleland* (Oxford, 2000), Rosalind Shaw, *Memories of the Slave Trade: Ritual and the Historical Imagination in Sierra Leone* (Chicago, 2002), Anne C. Bailey, *African Voices of the Atlantic Slave Trade: Beyond the Silence and the Shame* (Boston, 2005), and Sarah Nuttall and Carli Coetzee (eds), *Negotiating the Past: The Making of Memory in South Africa* (Cape Town, 1998). On past and present violence in southern Sudan, see Sharon E. Hutchinson, *Nuer Dilemmas: Coping with Money, War, and the State* (Berkeley, 1996), which is an outstanding example of historical anthropology. Another, on how the past is performed, is Karin Barber, *I Could Speak Until Tomorrow: Oriki, Women, and the Past in a Yoruba Town* (London, 1991). From a growing literature on witchcraft, broadly defined, try Luise White, *Speaking with Vampires: Rumor and History in Colonial Africa* (Berkeley, 2000), and Jean Allman and John Parker, *Tongnaab: The History of a West African God* (Bloomington, 2005). For a wide-ranging discussion of many of the issues raised here, see Paul Tiyambe Zeleza, *Manufacturing African Studies and Crises* (Dakar, 1997). Finally, two books on Africans in the world, past and present: Laurent Dubois, *Avengers of the New World: The Story of the Haitian Revolution* (Cambridge, Mass., 2004), and James Ferguson, *Global Shadows: Africa in the Neoliberal World Order* (Durham, NC, 2006).

Index

Index

Expand your collection of
VERY SHORT INTRODUCTIONS

Visit the
VERY SHORT INTRODUCTIONS
Web site

www.oup.co.uk/vsi

➤ **Information** about all published titles

➤ News of **forthcoming books**

➤ **Extracts** from the books, including titles not yet published

➤ **Reviews** and views

➤ **Links** to other **web sites** and main OUP web page

➤ Information about **VSIs in translation**

➤ **Contact** the editors

➤ **Order** other **VSIs** on-line

ANCIENT EGYPT
A Very Short Introduction
Ian Shaw

The ancient Egyptians are an enduring source of fascination – mummies and pyramids, curses and rituals have captured the imagination of generations. We all have a mental picture of ancient Egypt, but is it the right one? How much do we really know about this great civilization?

In this absorbing introduction, Ian Shaw describes how our current ideas about Egypt are based not only on the thrilling discoveries made by early Egyptologists but also on fascinating new kinds of evidence produced by modern scientific and linguistic analyses. He also explores the changing influences on our responses to these finds, through such media as literature, cinema and contemporary art. Each chapter deals with a different aspect of ancient Egypt, from despotic pharaohs to dismembered bodies, and from hieroglyphs to animal-headed gods.

http://www.oup.co.uk/isbn/0 19 285419 4

ARCHAEOLOGY
A Very Short Introduction
Paul Bahn

This entertaining Very Short Introduction reflects the enduring popularity of archaeology – a subject which appeals as a pastime, career, and academic discipline, encompasses the whole globe, and surveys 2.5 million years. From deserts to jungles, from deep caves to mountain tops, from pebble tools to satellite photographs, from excavation to abstract theory, archaeology interacts with nearly every other discipline in its attempts to reconstruct the past.

'very lively indeed and remarkably perceptive … a quite brilliant and level-headed look at the curious world of archaeology'

Barry Cunliffe, University of Oxford

'It is often said that well-written books are rare in archaeology, but this is a model of good writing for a general audience. The book is full of jokes, but its serious message – that archaeology can be a rich and fascinating subject – it gets across with more panache than any other book I know.'

Simon Denison, editor of *British Archaeology*

www.oup.co.uk/vsi/archaeology

ISLAM
A Very Short Introduction
Malise Ruthven

Islam features widely in the news, often in its most
militant versions, but few people in the non-Muslim
world really understand the nature of Islam.

Malise Ruthven's Very Short Introduction contains
essential insights into issues such as why Islam has such
major divisions between movements such as the Shi'ites,
the Sunnis, and the Wahhabis, and the central importance of the Shar'ia (Islamic law) in Islamic life. It also
offers fresh perspectives on contemporary questions:
Why is the greatest 'Jihad' (holy war) now against the
enemies of Islam, rather than the struggle against evil?
Can women find fulfilment in Islamic societies? How
must Islam adapt as it confronts the modern world?

> 'Malise Ruthven's book answers the urgent need for an
> introduction to Islam. ... He addresses major issues with
> clarity and directness, engages dispassionately with the
> disparate stereotypes and polemics on the subject, and
> guides the reader surely through urgent debates about
> fundamentalism.'
>
> **Michael Gilsenan, New York University**

www.oup.co.uk/isbn/0-19-285389-9

CHRISTIANITY
A Very Short Introduction
Linda Woodhead

At a time when Christianity is flourishing in the Southern hemisphere but declining in much of the West, this *Very Short Introduction* offers an important new overview of the world's largest religion.

Exploring the cultural and institutional dimensions of Christianity, and tracing its course over two millennia, this book provides a fresh, lively, and candid portrait of its past and present. Addressing topics that other studies neglect, including the competition for power between different forms of Christianity, the churches' uses of power, and their struggles with modernity, Linda Woodhead concludes by showing the ways in which those who previously had the least power in Christianity—women and non-Europeans—have become increasingly central to its unfolding story.

'her analysis is subtle and perceptive.'

Independent on Sunday

http://www.oup.co.uk/isbn/0-19-280322-0